Advance Praise

MW00617514

Full disclosure, Adriana Colotti and I are forever friends *and cocreators. We have a history of traveling and working together worldwide. We have always encouraged one another to express more of who we are. In this book Adriana wholeheartedly expresses and shares her unique wisdom. May you become more of who you are as you enjoy her presence!*

~ Peggy Phoenix Dubro

"My destiny is to build Bridges of Golden Light and share it for the greater good of all sentient beings". These words sum up the year-long labor of love I was privileged to share with Adriana during the birth of her book. This book is a journal, an invitation and a practical guide. It is Adriana's life experiences and journey of cosmic awareness. It is her invitation to recognize that we all are portals to the divine Source, two-way Bridge of Light between 'heaven and the marketplace', conduit of divine light and love to empower others. This book is also an amazing practical guide to help us live energetically aware, as we awaken to the truth that life is sacred and we are divine having a human experience. Adriana's dark night of the soul becomes the Bridge of Golden Light to wisdom, wonder, gratitude and loving service to others."

~ Maria M. Decsy

Dear Reader, you can with this remarkable book embark upon your own journey toward wholeness by exploring the wisdom principles shared by author Adriana Colotti Comel. Her life, her journey, is one of a profound seeker who never fails to be courageous in uncovering her personal secrets of the psyche, hers and ours. Universal wisdom teachings are available to all who dare to encounter aspects of the Self. Ms. Colotti dares and succeeds in unraveling complexities of consciousness, the Higher Self and the Soul. She shows, with her dedicated and determined seeking, that we all ultimately are on a path toward higher meaning, understanding and higher purposes in our lives whether we know it or not. Ms. Colotti certainly knows it. And her generous sharing of her process in self integration is uplifting indeed!

~ Shawn Randall

This spiritually illuminating book is a delight to read. It takes you on the author's journey of freedom and higher awareness. You will witness the gradual unfolding of an awakening that opened her to the mysteries of energy healing and enlightenment. The book is only part biographical, it is also a detailed exploration of higher wisdom that reveals hard won insights and understanding that can dramatically transform your life. It is written in an engaging style that weaves together story, explanation, and poetry into a seamless whole. The book itself is a spiritual journey that will take you through the inevitable darkness of human life into the exhilarating heights of divinity. In these pages you will discover the deeper significance and purpose of being here, on this planet, at the auspicious time. You are invited into a portal that leads to a higher dimension or reality where time and space do not exist. In that expansive space, you will become intimate with your deepest self and reflect on the purpose that is already beginning to shine through you. The wisdom of this book offers a loving framework through which a profound understanding of yourself and the world around you emerges. Please read this book as a spiritual practice. Each time you engage with it, allow the words to wash over you and gently unlock the mystery of human existence. As you read, the light of illumination will shine through the words leaving you inspired and uplifted.

~Jeff Carreira

Bridges of Golden Light

ISBN: 978-1-7358111-8-5

Mystery School Press
P.O. Box 63767
Philadelphia, PA 19147
mysteryschoolpress.com

Interior design by Sophie Peirce.

Printed in the United States of America.

Bridges *of* Golden Light

Multidimensional Experiences
My Piece of the Cosmic Puzzle

Adriana Colotti Comel

MYSTERY SCHOOL PRESS
Philadelphia, Pennsylvania

Preface

I AM the Particle, I AM the Wave

Relaxing in consciousness
I AM the bottom of the ocean
The wrinkles on the surface
The water of the flowing river
The tear rolling on my cheek
Abiding in consciousness
I expand and float
The joy of presence
The mystery of meditation
The Milky Way... my nervous system
Stars and neurons
I AM the particle, I AM the wave
Moving in the eternal moment
Everything is here, including me
I live in the space between the words,
in the silence between the breaths
I touch reality sinking into space
I transcend the corners of the soul
I organize files in consciousness, I feel clearer
I AM the particle, I AM the wave
In the sea of consciousness,
Sorting out, harmonizing, articulating
Sitting still I feel energized
My daily life is the same flow of meditation
Focused, inclusive, dancing with life
From the hub expanding concentric circles
As a pebble falling from above in a quiet lake

I access multidimensional layers of sensations
From the physical, emotional feelings
To the energetic and spiritual
Evolving a sensual experience of reality
The mystery of life unfolding
The body knows the secret is allowance
Spiraling in time, multiple points of light
Glide in my sensual encounter with life
As an enlightened galaxy touching eternity
Multicolored feelings, shades of light
The line between inner and outer space is blurry
I become intimate with myself and others
Where the presence of shared moments feels
delicious
Uniqueness dances with Interconnectedness
In the shifting relationship with the world
I AM the particle, I AM the wave
I feel as a rock in the river
caressed by the flowing water
Awareness observing, I am in the miracle now
Light flows from above and from the earth into
my core
I AM a bridge of light radiating
I reinvent myself in the process
Unexpected, Unimaginable, Magic,
I embrace uncertainty
I renew my unique expression
As the universe flows through me
Glimpses of the mystery unfolding
In a perennial dance
I hold the tension of the paradox

It feels like looking in a shattered mirror
Wanting to grasp multidimensionality
Radical acceptance of what is makes it whole
again
I find peace bridging the extremes now
I am the vessel of transformation
Open to Infinite Possibilities
Is "the other" the One asleep?
She is awakened by loving caresses of "the en-
lightened" One
They become One in the process
I dive into the complexity of sensations
I learn and feel lighter
I AM the particle, I AM the wave

~ Adriana Colotti Comel

Contents

CHAPTER ONE

The Book

———

Welcome, welcome.

This is an invitation to be the bridge of light you are, though you have probably never thought about it.

You see, I have spent the last 40 years of my life manually registering in a series of journals what we could call my spiritual life. Its evolution through the years is one of the things I am going to share in this book. I hope that you find inspiration in it and that we can keep each other company in what I call a spiritual life, a space for Spirit to come in and sustain a dialogue with you. A real conversation where you can share your states of mind, your fears, your worries, your pain and sorrow, your anxiety, your depression… and also your love, your joy, your beauty, your dreams and wishes, your creations and everything else you desire. It is like a best friend that listens and responds, that guides you always with infinite love and uttermost care.

My Brokenness vs. My Wholeness, The Dark Night of

the Soul, confronting the Dark One, the ascension after descending into the Shadows, and then Confused by the Light, the glimmering, shimmering reflection of the light on the flowing river is what mesmerizes me... the experience of brilliance that wraps me up... when I am there, I am that and I shine, and we shine together even more.

Then the Shadow shows up, my jealousy blows things up, the shadow of love and possessiveness, the attachment... I learned that love is universal, I dove in deep.

It all seems to be an individuation process, to find your voice, your light!

Discerning in the labyrinth of mirages the real thing, the raw real... we loved each other dearly and then he died on me, after wanting to kill me. All in one!

And I continue to learn: I owe nothing, not to him, not to my country, nor my parents or sister or friends... I owe nothing... guilt, shame, obligation?

I do exist, I do shine and I owe it to myself to be the brightest light I can be and be the Bridge of Golden Light that I AM. And so it is!

The journey began in my 20s, when psychoanalysis helped me reflect, cry out loud, shout, judge, criticize, complain (of course) about the state of the world... my world... and my relationships. These started with dysfunctional family ties, mainly with my mother, my father and my sister—they are still relevant, but over the course of these years I have found some closure.

I broke a spell with Mom. Her determination reshuffled the cards of my relationship with my sister. Jealousy was the card here too... Jealousy as a shadow, as an energy possession, as wanting to be the only one in the eyes of the Beloved... and when the Beloved is the Universe? Wanting to be the only one? The special one? After all, isn't it that we all only wanted to be loved?

This has been easiest with my father, as he has been gone for more than 18 years... and let me tell you, I have a much better relationship with him now than when he was alive. He is now my greatest angel, ever watching over me. I am open to his love and guidance that helps me to live my life fully and wisely.

I will share with you the loving relationships which in those times were important in my horizon. I will share my work through all my shadows and the shining light into the dark corners of my being to be able to love, be loved and move on in life.

You will find valuable lessons, Shadow Work, profound meditation and energy work: tools to help you live through turbulent times and come out the other side, enlightened and empowered.

There is much here about work, creativity and relationships, with both my seen and unseen friends: their guidance has been crucial for navigating the tumultuous times we live in. This is accompanied by poems as illustrative metaphors and inspirations for each step of the way of becoming, of being a Bridge of Light in your own life.

That is what the invitation is all about: be that light in your own life, learn to live an energetically aware life, connect and communicate with Spirit and be your own guidance for an evolutionary life without giving your power away to the social, cultural, family, religious conditioning of a paradigm that has forgotten the sacredness of life.

The way of talking, sharing and working with these things has also evolved. It is not easy to speak of this, and words are never enough to explain the multidimensional realities we live in as multidimensional beings. But they can bring you quite close. As for my own communications with Spirit, I name them spiritual poetry.

Dear beloved divine essence,
bridging with my universal self,
being the whole being,
Disentanglement of the voices that are oppressing me
I slip out of the entanglement and feel I fly
I go to the bottom of the ocean and bounce
back, flying over the horizon
I listen to all the voices…
It is the I AM that is listening
I am not one voice
I am the whole being
I am the One
I am the moon, not the finger pointing at the moon
AM I the moon?

Waltzer with Spirit

Dancing in the light
With grace coming in
I can see all the bridges of golden light
At first they are a curtain of thin filaments of
light that pour into nature coming from beyond
the veil…
Oh, but wait, this is quanta of light coming in
And I can see also quanta coming out…
The dance with Grace begun
And the two-way bridges of light are formed
And as floating awareness
You can enjoy the show with delight
It is a sacred spectacle
Where souls sing their songs
And waltz music from beyond plays in the
background
What a majestic feeling of sovereignty
When the Cosmos is all lit up
With stars and flowers alike
In the waltz with Grace
On the Bridges of Golden Light!!!
Thank You! What a joy and delight this is…

You are clearing the space for the new to come in. A long row of characters after bowing in gratitude, dismissed! To travel lighter, open space, the journey as a delight for newcomers to be welcomed!

Fleeting inspirations come as glimmers of light after my daily ritual to encounter my Higher Self. I go to the space where I meet with the Frequencies of

Golden Light that speak to me as I enjoy the warmth of the sunlight on a small bench by the river. The light shimmers over the flowing water, illuminating worlds of understanding and wisdom. I've called upon them and they are always there to communicate with me. There is an easy method that I use, taught to me by one of my unseen friends: Ask. Listen. And write. Each time I do this, and thus I have poured out my journals, a record of my journeys with my soul.

Dancing with the Energies

Bridging universes in a garden of growth to create beauty following the joy,
unforgetting what we are
Discovering poetry as a being without restrictions in the flow of cosmic imagination
what do we dare to imagine?
Dancing, swirling with the energies
Raising the frequency
Carving new tools and new ways of being,
wholeheartedly as the wise multidimensional beings we are
Increasing, raising, balancing consciousness
The lattice as our energetic skin—feeling energies
Microbiome around you and keeping a sense of Self
Freedom spirals as a new tool
I am as a unique expression of the universe
So we blossom

We are the third element
Unity to bridge the duality into wholeness
to evolve in this truth
Bridges of light
Dualities are up to us unique and united
Patterns of coherence
Brighter potentials

And this poem that speaks of what I do when…

Writing the Light

They see my portals in my writings…
The Universes and Galaxies are the entrance
to a new world of awe and majesty
opened up by the tenderness of a heart in nature
that beats to the rhythm of the Cosmos
The Interdimensional Bridges of Light
expand our consciousness in the intimacy of the
sacred
The caverns of the inside open up to the Milky
Way
transporting us to the wonder of life
Who is writing these journeys?
The extensive meadows are glimmering with the
sunshine
We become blinded by the light
Only to recognize the eternal brilliance of the
soul
Shimmering through oceans of gratitude
Of the Joy that comes just to be alive
Here and Now! Blessed be…

Or… the space of wonder…

The Color of the Leaves

The freshness of the forest
The clear circle in the sun
The peaking of her showing up with white garments
The bench in a garden-level dimension
Where there is the sparkling on the river
The chills of the encounter
Looking into it, stepping in, feeling the warmth
Where magic happens as the Bridge of Light is established
A dome of grace as a portal to other dimensions opens and I listen…
There is a tweet, a strong one that leads the way into the mystery
Calm reigns… I am in!
The color of the leaves reminds me that I love trees
They talk through us with a strong connection to the earth
Hugging them you have a grounding feeling
Photosynthesis…
Light made liquid…
Liquid light
Trees in their resilience, uniqueness and wisdom
The whispers of the winds of far unknown places
And what is real for us now when we hug them and know we are the same
A bridge between the earth and the stars

With many stories to tell and wisdom to share
Through the colors of the leaves...
Soul retrieval is real
Right relationship order
Individuation
We recover The Garden
We journey inside outside time into infinity
Speak to trees, rivers, mountains, spirit...
The house was on fire and in the ashes
I felt the heartbeat of the Universal tree
Secrets were revealed
Waking up with fresh water from the icy springs
of the mountaintop
I wash my eyes and there is clarity
Remembrance of the cavern where I retrieved
The diamond light crystals
As the treasured secret to access the soul
Crystal meditation sooths it
Restores oneness
Enlightens the dark and shadow spaces in
yourself
Illumine the corners of separation
Still in the womb of the earth, rivers flowing
Outside, the prairie full of purple and bright yel-
low daisies
Sunlight expressing through nature again
Wholeness in the warm womb of the earth
You belong to this galaxy
You are recognized among the stars and the hun-
dreds of galaxies as the shiny one
A planet in which light colors nature
Beauty is astounding!

The space and time for writing in my daily life is always a sacred moment, never casual: it involves the ritual of having a nice space on the couch (or even in my bedroom), always a candle, soft, soothing music and, of course, the invocation of the muse... I will also share with you the evolution of these rituals over the years, depending on the unseen friends that were stronger at that time. The listening, the writing and, of course, a cup of tea—green, generally, as this is my favorite. Each time it is magic: the hand starts to slide across the paper as though of its own accord, the warm and loving feeling permeates the room and I could go on forever...

A Cup of Tea

From the deep ground of Self
Where consciousness abides
Thoughts are as bubbles on the surface in boiling
water
They integrate into the whole
A new insight makes water hotter
Transformation occurs naturally
Water is the same water
Now, it has a new quality
It is warmer
When you drink the tea
Reintegration happens
You are clearer
Heart warms up and you expand
Just one sip...
What a miracle we are!

There is always a new revelation, considerations and reflections that blossom from each writing session. Sometimes, entries in the journal are a direct response to the question asked. Sometimes, poems flow into the paper as flowing water; surprises and revelations from other dimensions, other worlds, bridge through the writing into this reality... this moment... as words to be shared.

How Did the Book Come About?

I've been an energy worker for more than 20 years as a practitioner, a teacher and a teacher of teachers of the EMF Balancing Technique® (EMF = Electro Magnetic Field), created by Peggy Phoenix Dubro.

I have done much work with individual sessions, training practitioners, translating, traveling, doing on-line work and study collaborations. Hence, I developed a body of work that bridges energy work with conscious evolution, Shadow Work and meditation.

All of these experiences continued to evolve as a method of relating to students and clients alike, whereby my communication with Spirit, my writings, spiritual poetry and—of course—energy work always served as the foundational technique. To be a Bridge of Light with the divine, to reflect and empower others to be their own Bridge of Light with divinity, with others, with the world around them is huge transformational work. This change of perspective on life and reality brings profound changes in the lives of my clients and students.

Zen meditation was integrated into my life quite early, and it found a deepening and expansion in the Mystery School, founded by Jeff Carreira. Through my participation in the Members' Circle, I started to share the spiritual poetry that was rising more clearly within me; after a meditation retreat, it became clear to me that I needed to write a book. Jeff being a writer and a publisher, he immediately offered to publish it and continued to inspire me to go on with the project with his own teachings, writings and encouragement, for which I am very grateful.

Jeff once answered a question of mine saying that *of course* energy can talk to you. I felt so validated and grateful, as I have been doing that forever, communicating with and through energy… that gave me the impulse to continue with the endeavor of the book.

In general, channeling and working with energy is not something that people understand or validate. On the contrary: starting with my mother, my own family has always considered me a weirdo and denied any connection with energy. She said she didn't understand it, so… case closed.

With my daily meditation practice, my journaling, my channeling and energy work, my spiritual poetry and having solved the practicalities of daily life, I decided it was time to get my book done so that I could share with you, the reader, journeys, insights and tools that can illuminate you to live a more enlightened life indeed!

The whole story, my trajectory… where it all began.

I remember…
It all started with

Angelo di Dio
che sei il mio custode,
Illumina, reggi,
custodisci, e governa me,
che ti fui affidata
dalla pietà celeste

In English:
Angel of God,
you are my guardian,
enlighten me, hold me,
look after me, take care of me
who was entrusted to you
by heavenly piety
Amen

My mother taught me this little prayer as soon as I started to speak, and every night, on my knees with hands in prayer position, I looked at a beautiful angel image as I recited it since I was 2 years old… until now. I still remember.

From then on, I always knew the Universe had my back and I could trust life, listening to the whispers of my soul, which even in my darkest moments have appeared as streaks of golden light that magnetize me towards them. I had the courage, the determination, the love to be able to go forward… I am unsinkable… I am a Bridge of Light… from the Divine into the world... into my everyday life. Indeed!

Thank you, Mom!

There were two more episodes that set me on this path. These came when I was a teenager.

Wearing a black dress with red strawberries, I went out of the house to walk along the train tracks that were two blocks away. I felt a heavy soul, sadness pervading, and walked looking down at each step on the tracks. Suddenly, I looked up to the horizon in front of me and dazzled by a brilliant sun... I was walking in the light, going forward into infinity... my path to infinity was established. The darkness and the heaviness lifted away, and I continued walking on the tracks, which led me to a very busy street in the big city where I lived. I returned home with a new perspective of where I was going in life.

The other episode was a Sunday, when we were called to church. *Really?*, I thought. I always had better things to do that were more fun. I went anyway, and in the middle of mass, when it was time to make peace, I could see the hypocrisy of it all. People I knew hated each other outside, who hurt, criticized and judged each other harshly, were there wishing peace upon each other... for me, that was it. I wasn't going to play that game anymore. It was cynical, not true, they did not mean it, it was all theatrical to be forgotten as soon as mass was over. It reminded me of when Jesus chased the traders away from the temple. My relationship with God could not be based on the deception of being good. My search for truth, authenticity and transparency began that day as I left mass, never to return.

My quest to establish a real, truthful relationship with God was not going to be enclosed in a church: it was going to be out there in life, in nature, in the eyes of the people. I also knew that it had to be away from a home that restricted me with social, cultural, family and religious conditioning and felt like a prison. I was determined to set myself free and to begin an authentic search for a true God that was not enclosed behind walls.

Leaving my parents' home, I immediately began my incursion into other dimensions of spirit. In my early 20s, over 3 years I experimented with cannabis and had very interesting revelations about the Universe as a Cosmic Spiral. This, of course, could be dismissed at the time as mere hallucinations.

What happened instead is that by registering all of those revelations and choosing to interpret them as expanded knowledge given to me by a broader field of consciousness that I could access through the relaxation generated by the cannabis, it developed into the very basis of the energy work I do now and have done for more than 20 years, helping hundreds of students and clients with structured quantum physics energy work: the EMF Balancing Technique®. I will always be grateful for this technique, as it opened me up to live energetically aware and thus be an effective tool in the service of others.

I explored and practiced in the shamanic world: Mexico has long and ancient traditions in this realm, and this continued to open me up to other dimensions of being: without knowing or naming it, I was exploring my own multidimensionality, indeed!

My loving relationships were, of course, also very rich experiences. At some point, they led me to believe I was writing a book with my journaling and psychoanalysis treatment called *Mirages—Mirrors—Reflections*. That book never came to fruition, but all my romantic relationships have been a profound deepening on the essence of love and the human experience that always led me to understand and love myself more. I learned to live with myself, strengthening my love for divinity and bringing that back to everyday life.

As a sociologist, I wrote a community theater play for cultural promoters in the poorest areas of the country. I had a job in the Secretariat of Education, which allowed me to work with Indigenous groups to develop programs in different areas of the country... a beautiful, fun and creative program. I wrote and directed 3 community theater plays that then went itinerant all over the country to bridge educational programs for the poorest of the poor, including prison inmates.

Ceramics was my incursion into the artistic realm, which I loved and continue to love dearly. The alchemy of earth, water, air and fire involved in the magic of making a piece from scratch is amazing. The essence of the process of creation and the fire in the kiln having the last word is always astounding. This was another piece of the cosmic puzzle and another deepening into the multidimensional being that I AM. Delightful!

My channeling experience started relatively early

in my life, as I was invited to participate in workshops and channeling lessons with the wonderful teacher and trance channel Shawn Randall. She channels a wise and loving consciousness who calls himself Torah. The two specialize in an in-depth approach to personal and spiritual development, and they have taught the art of channeling since 1984. Channeling offers a multidimensional point of view of all that we are and all that we do. We are much more than we know!

Through the personal sessions and the translations I did for Shawn's Spanish-speaking clients, I developed a strong relationship with Torah. Ever since, I have been channeling for myself with the method that they taught me: ask, listen and write. And it has worked for me to this day. I started with my Divine Dragon of the Light (which, by the way, is also the name of the ceramic sculpture I made of it), and I went on with Cascade, Ezekiel and the Evolutionary Bridges. The latter then became Bridges of Light and are now the Frequencies of Golden Light that I channel: the Bridges of Golden Light that brought me to you with the book of the same title, written and structured with their help.

I had a solid foundation of mental discipline, acquired after 10 years of practicing Zen buddhist meditation with 3 or 4 sesshins (intensive retreats) a year in the Rochester Zen Centre with Roshi Philipp Kapleau and with Sensei, his Dharma heir. And after also being leader of Casa Zen in Mexico City for two years I was highly prepared for what Carter Phipps and Jeffrey Kripal call the Sociology of the Paranormal.

I worked for 6 years with Roger Lachance, originator of the Lachance method of emotional release. This was an incursion into working with the paranormal, the interdimensional and esoteric phenomena as worlds that interpenetrate and cross over. This is where I started properly with energy work.

Later on, I found Peggy Phoenix Dubro, the originator of the EMF Balancing Technique®, through Kryon (a loving angelic entity). If you go to kryon.com, you will find that this website is an esoteric spiritual site featuring information from Kryon, channeled by Lee Carroll—the original Kryon channel, who has been doing this work since 1989. (The word "Kryon" has been used in the last few years by many others in various forms; Lee is not affiliated with any of them and only does his own channeling, transmitting his own teachings and uplifting messages from Kryon.)

With Peggy, I learned the technique that I still offer today as the first module of a Bridge of Light with your inner wisdom. It became the first step for the body of work that I call Bridges of Light, which I will explain in this book as profound Energy Psychology work.

Journaling has been a constant during all these incursions.

Paradigm Shifting

This is another topic that runs throughout the book: as I learned with Jeff Carreira, the paradigm shift will come out of seeing ourselves as the source of consciousness. This was new language for me: even though I had been studying, reading and participating in summits and workshops of an evolutionary kind, this nailed it for me.

In the Mystery School, I have been surrounded by people anchored in consciousness and with shared activities such as daily meditations, retreats, discussions and Jeff's teachings and guidance. Additionally, there is reading sacred text, nurturing with healthy food to keep the system light and clear to feel physically good working with your soma and feeding your soul periodically. All of this would be conducive to this paradigm shift and a plus to my spiritual life.

Reading Jeff's books, including his transdimensional fiction novels, has been a huge inspiration that keeps me going. It keeps me believing that another way of life is possible for me, for us, at this time in this world and it is a constant validation of what I am doing. Infinite Gratitude!

This continues to be part of the invitation presented in this book.

Giving birth to higher dimensional realities in the ordinary world is the passion of an artist of possibility. I learned this from Jeff, and it is expressed below in my own writing:

Dear Beloved Divine Essence
Bridging with my Universal Self
Being the Whole Being
I am Homo Amor

I pray... God listens. I am expressing in daily life what I have as guidance: my access to higher dimensions and my dive into pure awareness every morning allow me to permeate my life with depth and meaning and Everything is included.

I am learning what it means to live multidimensionally. All is included, and I choose to put my attention here or there to create the reality needed to continue the flow of life and expansion into wider realms of creative expression.

An image I get constantly these days is that of concentric circles, both within and outside of me. I have these judgments of right and wrong. That bothers me... what do I need to choose at any moment in order to be in the flow of divine guidance, regardless of what happens or presents itself?

How to live in a new paradigm? This is a challenge for me now, and there are specific matters that need to be tended to; it is always interactive, related with other... others... as there is an interdependence to be dealt with all of the time. I need help to flow easily through all the challenges I encounter; they show me what I am holding on to. I am aware that I am aware of that. Pure awareness does not judge, and I want to act from there. There are higher purposes.

There is a divine pool of awareness to dive into and manifest from there a new reality that grows and blooms...

Center Below... Center Above... Radiate Core

What a mystery life is... I am interested in this mystery

Practice of No Problem

Conscious Contentment

Being the awareness that is aware

And now, how to live and bring from that dimension into the minutiae of daily life the feedback of the mysterious void of galaxies and stars that are part of these expanded universe?

Focus like a laser light into the depth of reality and create expansively and freely a new way of living life in a creative and joyful way.

What an exciting proposition… indeed!

Artist of Possibility: Bringing a New Paradigm to Life

"Emergence Education publishes an online journal that continually presents articles, interviews, art and poetry that express and explain the emerging possibilities of a new paradigm. In our pages you will find information about the ideas, people and perspectives that are catalyzing new ways of seeing, feeling and acting in the world."

This is the way Jeff Carreira presents this very well-done online journal, and I feel honored by the presence in almost every issue of a poem of mine.

"Each issue of The Artist of Possibility will include the voices of some of today's most respected paradigm shifting luminaries, as well as contributions by members in The Mystery School."

Quoting Jeff:

"You are the exact expression of cosmic creativity that you were born to be"

"You are full of possibilities"

I decided that with this book I am contributing with the piece of the puzzle I was born to illuminate. And here I am, paraphrasing Jeff as I take notes of the many teachings, conferences and everything else he is always offering in many formats, as he himself is a prolific artist of possibility. Allowing ourselves to act as a conduit, these possibilities begin to filter through us in infinite ways: artistic projects, writing, scientific illumination, entrepreneurial adventure… What matters is that what is brought through is coming from a dimensionality beyond the ordinary: we are training for a process of creative illumination! The existent possibilities of other dimensions to draw this potential in, filter them through whatever creative process and whatever creative medium we are drawn to bring them into manifestation in ways that can inspire others… they see another dimensional possibility, a portal. That kind of art has the capacity to transport someone's consciousness to the place the art came from and give them access to the same potential, and this is our role in changing the world, in bringing a new paradigm into being. Through it, we learn to love both the form and the formless.

That is what the Artistry of Possibility is: Creative Illumination.

At the end of this book, you will find a list of all the websites and books by various teachers that have been the Bridges of Light I made. They are part of the wisdom practices and sessions, teachings and offerings from my body of work and references to the websites that have nurtured my journey. I hope they serve as tools of inspiration and encouragement for you as they have been for me.

Neal Donald Walsch, author of the *Conversations with God* book series, said: "I am a sorcerer… not only the source…" So I am writing to bring future possibilities into presence, to articulate a new paradigm, an intuition of a way of being so you get inspired to bring your piece of the cosmic puzzle too, expanding your multidimensional experiences through any means of creative illumination.

The book is a Bridge of Light in itself, with chapters as building blocks for the Bridge of Light you are. As reality is a co-creative act we participate in, here we are co-creating impossible possibilities beyond the current paradigm and articulating a new reality in words to be manifested in all the shades of light we are as creative human beings.

The book is a journey and an invitation. A journey of the idea of cosmic awareness flowing through me into the world through the language of energy, light, Golden Frequencies and an invitation to become the Bridge of Light you also are.

All of this is told through direct experiences with students and clients in my more than 20 years of work as a practitioner, teacher and teacher of teachers of the EMF Balancing Technique® and stories and specific cases with which you are going to be able to relate and benefit for your own growth.

The contemplation of my past as a Bridge of Light has healed me and confirmed a whole new purpose of joy and love from a life lived authentically in each moment as a wholehearted, multidimensional, wise being I am, as the expression of cosmic consciousness.

For me, writing the book is an act of generosity and a call to share what is significant for me in living an authentic, enlightened life. It is my contribution to what is needed for a change of paradigm in our daily lives.

Like an astronaut training for a flight in space, we need to deepen our understanding and realization of love. You travel through the quagmires of your ego structure to universalize yourself and be the bridge with your Universal Self!

If you are reading this, it is because you have the courage it takes to make that journey. Thank You for being here and I hope you read between the lines that offer the spaciousness and dimensions of your own journey as a Reflection of your own light. We will do Alchemy together, alchemy understood as the art and science of converting the life energy of the Cosmos into a well-lived human life... in this case, yours.

You will find that the book is a way to access answers and tools for your most pressing questions and hurdles to gain clarity and illumination into your next step in your evolutionary process.

Becoming a Bridge of Light is a process. This book is a guide (rather than steps) for becoming, of how it happened for me and how it can happen for you.

I wrote the book all along with my practice and teaching, it is an invitation into a space where we Rewire.

Rewiring

I wonder if our multidimensionality is to have many experiences of different dimensions at the same time...

I sit and have the experience of me, my body, the environment and at the same time I am a laser light stimulating my neurons in the synapsis process

generating little big bangs in each neuron that communicate this light through all of the points of light in the brain with connectivity in all cells of the body

The junk DNA activates and reveals the awareness of the ages through me

All layers of DNA, all dimensions are activated with the rewiring of my brain in a huge big bang explosion that awakes as me. Here and Now.

This is the magic of been connected, transformed, alive, electrical.

I feel content and at peace experiencing the miracle of being alive.

A constant celebration of light and awareness that continues in each moment of our existence where we have the privilege to be the witnesses of this multidimensional reality that has no boundaries

We manifest the power of our imagination in real moments of enlightenment where we can say we are transformed by the light...

Expanded... rewired...

One foot in this world and the other in multidi-mensionality, bringing it down, percolating, bridging into this reality and sharing it with others, revelations revealed in the book. The energy is pouring through you, you feel the life in your body-mind-heart.

Life is flowing through you, a portal between the external world and its source. The sun warms us up and is the light, and we can see the colors and vibrations of our world.

We are the portals to the source!

A Bridge of Light!

All is Well

Weaving threads of light
Meshing in the now
The myriad of events that brought me to this
moment
and will take me to a glorious future
The wisdom that has come from the giving and
receiving
The glorious moments of presence
Where galaxies explode into multiple realizations
The glory and grace to be content and alive
Discovering the ways of what is right for me to
do in life
Exploring and finding out the face of
opportunity
in every moment that arises in consciousness
A splendid way to follow your path of
expression,

manifestation and contribution to the whole of
existence
Coming from the wholehearted trust that All is
well in the Universe
and it could not have been any other way
Simple and rich at the same time
it is bewildering when you can see eternity in a
well lived present moment
The confluence of all of your life and
the becoming in the here and the now
The perspective is wide, open, huge
The celebration is intense
The enthusiasm is explosive
Everything that has transpired until now makes
total sense
Good sense!
Hallelujah!
I can see colored fireworks everywhere
From a peaceful and joyous perspective
Blessed to be alive and well
All is well in the Universe!
And so it is!

Through the journey of self-discovery, we resonate
with our spiritual self and with others… the chapters
are:
- The Book
- The Bridges of Light
- The Blending
- The Relationships
- The Energy Work

- The Body of Work
- The Multidimensionality

So, in reading the book you are already experiencing an energy session, each time you come into this dome of light of no space and no time and you access your own multidimensionality and me functioning as a facilitator of your own empowerment as I shine through you Frequencies of Golden Light that allow your own inner wisdom to readjust your own energy as you need it.

You can go through the book in an orderly way or you can look for specific guidance in one of the chapters, or else every time you are meant to find your own answers as it is meant to be a dialogue with your own expanded consciousness that allows you to reflect on the path of your own life.

The chapters dive into what we do understand as the multidimensional aspects of Bridges of Light, discovering and becoming more of who you are. Indeed!

So... we bridge Enlightenment and Endarkenment, concluding with Engoldenment. These are the terms used by Andrew Harvey, founder and director of the Institute for Sacred Activism (an international organization focused on addressing contemporary crises by becoming inspired, effective and practical agents of systemic change for peace and sustainability through deep spiritual knowledge, courage, love and passion).

Resonating...

Resonating with higher vibrations of the awak-
ened Cosmos
Where softs winds of change blow eternally
With the speed of light
We are showered by trillions of stars
As dots of brilliant light coming through us
We merge with awakening consciousness
through eons of time
In the expansiveness of being One with the
Cosmos
The peace and emptiness of the freedom within
comes from vibrating with higher frequencies of
light
Golden glimmering vibrant light
As a pool percolating through multi-universes
reaching a blue planet, our temporary home
In resonance we meet through the expansive feel-
ing of a sacred space
shaped as our body of light that materializes as a
human being
The expression of the dream of the source of
creation
In luminous colored frequencies
In a unique concert of united selves!
Indeed!

A book of congruence, written in integrity from
the depth of my being, from the truth of my soul,
surrendering to what life wants from me, a book my
soul was meant to write, my legacy. Writing, trusting

the flow, in resonance with my soul as a contribution to humanity with my unique perspective, surrendered to my soul's purpose.

My piece of the Cosmic Puzzle!

In Gratitude and Celebration!

Adriana

CHAPTER TWO:

The Bridges of Light

———

This is not a linear process or a straight path of awakening that I can draw for you. The only thing I can do is offer you my experience of what worked for me to live a more enlightened life and be a facilitator for this in your own process through the different options I offer as a practitioner, as a teacher and now across the doors that will continue to open with this book.

Each of my poems is a breakthrough. They are Bridges of Golden Light through which I name the unknown from the Divine into the human realm of expression and back, downloading higher energies into the warmth of open hearts willing to listen, bridging mind and heart into a melting pot of the energy of love to journey back into the unknown. Quite an adventure it is, indeed! A spicy soup adding flavor to my life… and to yours, if you allow it to! A language of the soul into divinity and back to the human realm! A Bridge of Light, a two-way street! Soul manifesting divinity through me and sharing it for our journey of awakening in my understanding of the way Jeff Carreira so clearly put it.

The notion of a Bridge of Light started for me when I was working with Barbara Marx Hubbard and her sister Patricia Ellsberg in a 2016 workshop in which the former's book *Emergence—The Shift from Ego to Essence* was the working material. It was very significant in my spiritual development: having done energy work for more than 16 years with the EMF Balancing Technique®, I was bridging this work of energetically-aware living with that of Barbara's "Conscious Evolution."

My body of work was thus evolving as a bridge between the EMF Balancing Technique® and Conscious Evolution. So after a First Module of the 12 sessions of the Technique®, I offered my students and clients to accompany them with a Second Module of 12 sessions bridging the energy work with Emergence, followed by a Third Module that continued to bridge that energy work with another book by Barbara, which I translated into Spanish: *52 Codes for Conscious Self-Evolution—A Process of Metamorphosis to Realize Our Full Potential Self.*

I now had 3 Modules of 12 sessions each, where I bridged the work of energy of the EMF with the work of Emergence and Conscious Evolution. More on this follows in the next chapters: how my body of work continued to grow, and the different bridges you can follow in your own spiritual development.

As I said, this sprang from my own spiritual development and work, which was also an answer of support to those clients that wanted to continue to deepen the work we had begun with the energy calibration sessions of the EMF Balancing Technique®.

I needed to name what I was doing and to share it with students, clients and whomever else wanted to know more about it, so my website was born. *Puentes de Luz*, it was called (Bridges of Light in Spanish). It presented this invitation:

> *Infinite compassion and grace for all that has transpired*
> *In the personal and the collective*
> *Our vision strained from logic's sight*
> *Is refreshed with the dew of the heart*
> *Falling into calm, deep knowing States,*
> *Capable of loving more and embracing compassion,*
> *Listening to whispers of the soul*
> *And knowing we are never alone.*
> *Let inner wisdom spread and manifest*
> *In all our deeds as we build Bridges to the Heart.*
>
> *Forgive, Dear God, the craziness of our world,*
> *Enlighten our souls so we can hold eternity in the present moment,*
> *Awaken us to the truth that we are divine, that life is sacred and we are all interconnected in one web of life.*
> *Help us be beacons of light for the dark night of the soul*
> *So we can reflect the radiance at the core of our beings to illuminate the path.*

*Help us, Dear God, assist those who are awakening
to the divine impulse of creation within
So together, in resonance, we can build Bridges of
Light to comfort and uplift our conflicted world...
Be a Bridge of Light*

Then I understood... it is the holding of the tension between the passionate intent and the absolute and radical acceptance of what is at the same time that draws the flowing shades of light that is the path of the miraculous. I have been wholeheartedly devoted to the journey of awakening! I have been a Bridge of Light from the beginning: first bridging the different paths I had already explored and evolving my body of work, then realizing that is what I was with all my poems and writings... and now with this book, which draws from all the uninterrupted journaling I have done since 1983 to register my journey home.

My comments, reflections and writings come from the field of awareness as an expression of the divine flowing through me to empower another. This has been my journey with the Universal Calibration Lattice®—a system in our energy anatomy, a hyperspatial and inter-dimensional construct, nowadays known as the toroid of consciousness named by its originator: Peggy Phoenix Dubro, my beloved teacher whom I met in the year 2000 and who taught me the first steps of the EMF Balancing Technique®. I continued learning it with her and still do to this day, and it became my lifestyle: living energetically aware from that point on, when I became a practitioner, a teacher and teacher of teachers of this work.

Now, I expand my work as Bridges of Light that continue to develop as I go along with my practice, my teachings and my writing. I have always enjoyed my journaling and use it as a main tool in my sessions with clients. It is a contemplation that turns into a flow in another dimension, where I access the awareness that is aware and I can translate it for another. Actually mirroring from my core to another's core, it becomes an expansive dance in the flow of life.

The in-betweenness is the bridging of my Universal Self with my Essence. The intention of transformation is the surrender to the Divine, to be expressed clearly into my daily life and the relationship with others and the world.

I am delicately weaving the messages from the realm of the unknown so they can be translated into creative acts of illumination of reality through a third language with others, empowering them to live their most enlightened lives.

Developing the Bridging of Light

Now I understand what I was doing then, back when I followed the trainings of the EMF Balancing Technique®. Where I came from, in all my years of energy work and journaling, diving into the deep realm of Spirit, through all of my relationships and processing, I have learned this:

Becoming my whole being each day

Allowing the sunlight to warm me
To shine on my sad and hurt places
And enlighten the darkness and the doubt
Allowing frozen waters to melt and flow free
To integrate with the stream of golden light
Dancing in me now
So seeds of possibility might bloom
And express their beauty and care for all life
Decoding the meaning of divine love
In every interaction
And the miracle in each moment

This was my way of living, and it continued to develop with these same principles as I evolved.

It became even clearer after listening to Barbara read her Evolutionary Sacrament at the end of the Sacred Journey class and workshop that many of us shared.

Emerging Evolutionary

I can feel the expansion of my heart
And in every cell of my body
In every layer of DNA
Every fiber of light within me
I love myself divinely
For I am Divine
And use my divinity
To steer me to the safe harbors of life
My Essential Self
My Soul Codes
My Life Purpose,

All reflecting wholeness
As a bridge of light within
Bridging with the light of others
As a Universal vibration
In the field of light
Warmth expands in my body
Arousal of co-creation
Courage and trust in the process
Embracing the wounded
Feeling at home
On the path of Emerging Evolutionary
In the Energy of love
Towards the planetary awakening!
And so it is!

And so the path was clear to follow and that is what I did and continue doing as the Bridge of Light I AM that I AM... indeed!

This was only 2015 and there was a weird thing that happened with time. Real time is not linear; I would call it your soul time, as for the soul there are many lifetimes and this is the one that you happen to be in now... so no ordinary time nor space. The dome of timelessness and spacelessness that forms as soon as I start a balancing session with a client... or when I say my opening rituals in the morning to posture my energy for journaling, contemplation or writing... slipping into another dimension of being, as the multidimensional being that I AM... it's like a portal to other dimensions.

Nowadays, I directly call the Vibratory Frequencies

of the Bridges of Golden Light that softly speak warmly through me and I transcribe onto the blank pages of beautiful journals with lovely art on the cover. They inspire me to write profusely by hand with the violet ink of my favorite energel pen.

I have been doing this every day for many, many years now. Time is just a convention… real time is my multidimensional life, which I enjoy immensely! Indeed!

Bubbling Up…

Like the spherical fireworks
The bubbling up of myriad experiences
Arising in consciousness
In our encounter with life
It is an ongoing and unending
Dance with life…
Worlds and dimensions traveled by
Each of the bubbles of the spring
A common spring as Source for All
Individual expressions of the One
Colorful explosions of sensations
That inhabit the canvas of this lifetime
Jumping off to other encounters
of unknown dimensions
A reminder of a vast Cosmos we float in
Transported in from the inside out
Or is it from the outside in?
We are the bubbles of the Universe
that reflect light of Source

Unto each bubble that rose up from Source
All in One unending sensation of Life.

In Love

Awake, Aware, Conscious
I AM Awareness
Always have been, am and will be
I AM Content
I call it to be a Bridge of Light
I see all of us as Bridges of Light, indeed!
So… we are from the stars and from the earth
A unique expression of awareness
The Infinite Field
Manifesting our uniqueness
The lake, the ocean, the air we breathe;
The concentric circles of the pebble falling into
the lake,
The waves of the surface of the ocean
The rainbow is per excellence the bridge of light
It has all the shades of light that color the arc of
its ephemeral existence
Appears from nowhere, ends nowhere, though
we can see a trajectory
Shades of light
Uniqueness in the sky
We interact like that and build more bridges
between us
It is a colorful symphony we play
Everyone plays its note in a unique way
Shining the light of awareness
It is the same light for all, the Source

The softness of my awareness is translucent
It warms me up in the contentment of being
alive
As the miracle I was waiting for
It is a wonderful mystery contemplating itself
Another bridge of light from the Infinite to the
Finite ecstasy of this moment
So intimate and yet eternal
How can I not be In Love with awareness?
It is all there is.

Not Only a Metaphor

At this point, when I was able to relate to the Bridges of Light not only as a body of work but as my soul path and, later, as the Frequencies of Light with which I communicate, I started to find validation in synchronicities all around me and interpret events, studies and situations in my own life with a more amplified light. It definitively expanded my vision, my understanding of life itself as a sacred process.

I constantly find confirmation. For example: in one of her conferences, Lynne McTaggart an award-winning journalist and author consistently voted one of the world's top 100 spiritual leaders, affirms that the real language of the human body is frequency, that all human beings are communicating via light… within them and between them…

My heart jumped when I heard these things. For me, it is the perfect description of being Bridges of Light, not only as a poetic articulation but as the real thing. I can see this everywhere I look with my multi-dimensional eyes.

She went on to say that there are bio-photons, tiny currents of ordered light from our DNA, and that this is the most coherent light in nature. Light waving at the same light in the same amplitude. Together acting as a giant wave as the signal gets stronger. She said we are sending and receiving, signaling to our environment in a Morse code of light emissions. We are light beings communicating with our environment at every moment. We are energy systems. We are beings of energy of light…

This confirms my own experience in my many years of energy work: it is my belief that we are spiritual/light energy beings having a human experience. From biology to thoughts to the environment and beyond, giving and receiving light and energy. I've always known this, since 2000 when I started to learn the EMF Balancing Technique®, working with the human electromagnetic field and living energetically aware, learning, practicing and teaching this… for more than 20 years now.

I remember past experiences in which my light communications were present—they always have been—and my poetry registered the in-between states of enlightenment and the bridges between my higher self and the Light Frequencies with which I communicate, as well as how it all started… being the Bridge of Light between the stars and the earth, with a gift for reflecting core-to-core and the almost detective-like ability to not settle until what is in every interaction or situation is revealed to enhance the truth that underlies the experience of reality as is.

The help of unseen friends like Torah enhanced my channeling and confidence greatly, as did the beautiful building blocks crafted with the courses and meditations that are helping put together my cosmic puzzle... indeed! The invaluable experience given to hundreds of people with my sessions and myriad personal interactions helped me grow and develop my gift of being a Bridge of Light, bringing more of the divine into everyday life and really helping others develop the same qualities to be Bridges of Light in their own lives, allowing grace to activate the wisdom, the love, the joy of life into their own ordinary lives and their interaction with others. This is an invaluable quality that I have developed, and it brings me to the point of hearing and heeding the call to extend my gift and publish a book with the invitation to become, to activate the Bridge of Light that each one of us is for our own lives... and to build Bridges of Light in the energy of love with others in every aspect of life, with relationships being the only way for a planetary awakening in love, for the real change of paradigm that is so necessary in this troublesome world we live in, where most people have forgotten the sacredness of life indeed!

There is a desperate need to shift paradigms and be—become—the artists of possibility in the creation of a new world where we are able to live in harmony and reconnect with nature as the superhumans we are, with humility and compassion... to be better humans with the help of technology as a tool, not the dominant force of evolution; coming from the energy of the human heart, bridging our minds and hearts to build a more enlightened world indeed!

We are weaving the realm of the known with the unknown/the ordinary and the extraordinary/the divinity and the everyday life. Hold the tension!

Radiating Core Energy Exercise

Take a few deep breaths. Throughout this exercise, each step is associated with deep, long breaths.

You call to your Center Below. You visualize a sphere of golden light 60cm (24in) below your feet and golden light flowing down your core from your Center Above, which is another sphere of golden light 60cm (24in) above your head—your connection with higher energies, higher knowledge.

This flow of golden energy through your core flows down to the Center Below to connect with the energies of the earth. We start the magic of activating the Bridge of Light we are. We come from the stars and are of the earth. With the power of your imagination and visualization, you activate the magic in you.

After a few moments, when you can feel a connection with the energy of the earth through your Center Below, you call to your Center Above. Now you visualize how the flow of golden energy ascends from the Center Below through the Core to your Center Above. We have established the Bridge of Golden Light. We connected the higher energies with the energies of the Earth and back. A two-way Bridge of Golden Light.

Now we say (out loud if possible): "Radiate core." What you are visualizing is a column of golden light radiating to all of your universe as you know it.

Now, you stop and feel the expansion. Indeed!

This is the Bridge of Light, you are expansively accessing your own galaxies to shine your light into the darkness of the world, which needs a reflection to transcend the blind spots and implement the reign of the loving heart!

Radiating Light

Holding the tension means bridging the tension of opposites in your own wisdom: you bridge with the light and you bridge with the dark and you come out the other side unified. It is a third language of energy. You stand in your power as a Bridge of Light and allow the bright light of the inner wisdom to enlighten your life, your truth.

Whatever stage, age, crisis or situation you are in, you can always access your inner wisdom with the different tools presented here to gain more clarity in your evolutionary transformational process. It is an alchemical process, not unlike Hermes Trismegistus's search for truth and knowledge—the "philosopher's stone"—and the transformation of different metals into gold. "As above, so below, as within, so without, as the universe, so the soul." As Bridges of Light, we hold the tension, we calibrate, we enlighten our shadows and we transform. After all, darkness is only the absence of light.

We are here to resacralize the world, to repair and restore our tired and weary world, starting with "transcending the brokenness within ourselves and that entails a personal transformation that is key to our ability to help transform the world. It takes a journey without distance from the head to the heart," as Marianne Williamson says.

We change perspective and transform—indeed!—from the inside out, not the other way around.

A passionate intent and a radical acceptance of what is are a paradoxical confluence meeting bridge that creates the opening through which miracles happen. Hold the tension! And allow yourself to be the Bridge of Light to illuminate the dark corners, the blind spots in the individual and collective spaces. Be that lighthouse for yourself and others!

There are lattices upon lattices: one is the lattice of who you are in the moment as an individual; the second lattice is your core energy, the core of your infinite being; the third lattice is made of those bridges between the individual I and the Infinite I, where the archetypical male and female energies merge as the archetype of universal partner or the Beloved.

The Bridges of Golden Light are in-between frequencies that allow the healing and integration to happen.

Infinity Loop

You can continue with your visualization and the power of your imagination, wrapping yourself up in a huge infinity loop of golden energy that you draw all around you with your right hand. Its center is at your belly button and it extends from your Center Below to your Center Above. You breathe deeply and relax into it, feeling the expansion… indeed!

A Balanced Cross

It is a constant flow of energy, an exchange between the higher energies and the energies of the earth flowing through us. They intersect at your heart and then you discover there is yet another exchange of energy at a horizontal level, between the energies of giving through the right and of receiving through the left. You now visualize a balanced cross.

We are a miracle. To go beyond is to accept the giving and receiving of this flow of love from top to bottom and from bottom to top, from right to left and back.

Thus, an intense flowing system of energy and light forms the bridge of grace with which we are journeying through a world of marvel and chaos. The beyond is inclusive, and we can bring it to the center of the infinity loop—the know knot—where all the ancient knowledge is revealed and we can discover ourselves as the impulse of evolution itself with millions of years flowing through us as us expressing here and now forever.

This is the mystery we are, and the beyond is to realize that there are no limits of time and space when we are open to receive the flow of love that is the universe itself as us and through us.

Here is where abundance is made clear and we can rest in trust and confidence, assured that there is no problem. We will ever be provided and we will expand as the flow of the universe itself. "Rest assured that victory is yours." This is what Barbara Marx Hubbard taught me, bless her soul!

A Healing

I feel an emptiness in my guts, in the rings of light of my plexus. The hiatal hernia dissolves as the struggle and effort that generated it fades, along with the idea that life is hard, that it is a struggle, that I need to make a depleting effort just to barely make it… that is what produced it.

Healing strings of golden light, fibers and infinity loops of golden energy are vibrant, electrical and transformative flowing through me, giving to me, returning me to my original state of grace where I am creative and excited about possibility in my life. The traumas of my ancestors remain in the past and are not part of me; I see and know that I can be compassionate towards them, as they have a world view that cannot understand mine, will reject or exclude or resist mine.

My mother and I agreed on the fact that we disagreed in almost everything that is important. From there, we made a new start that let me relate to her in the limited way I could… no expectations. This allowed me to soar and expand and look for joining genius somewhere else.

I do not force it... I accept. It still hurts: it is bitter, painful, disappointing and... this is ego stuff... nothing to do with me. As from the ground of being, I can accept what is and soar beyond.

I am starting to see how the talents and gifts I have are starting to weave together to manifest and express further as a unity of creation where we can join genius and create the paradigm shift needed to prevail as the vibrant light in my life that makes my heart sing.

This is the flow... the creative flow I am interested in cultivating and developing.

This is exciting and helps me shine my light through those cracks in the layers of thick mud that accumulated with every disappointment.

Cracks in the Soul

Cracks in the Soul?
There are none.
Wholeness has no cracks!
What a release!
This moment is Perfect.
I AM whole!

This shows me that the inner light is still shining and burning with a luminosity that blinds and can permeate the rest of my universe.

I am updating my operating system, healing old traumas, meditating and journaling it through to come out the other side renewed and hopeful again.

Writing about these fleeting moments when my

insights of truth and hope arise is a way of communicating to myself and others and build those Bridges of Light, streams of communication and sharing that allow for an intimate creative and profound conversation to take place.

Healing took place! Infinite Gratitude, indeed!

A Process of Becoming and Being a Bridge of Light

You started the journey with this tool of energy for evolution, to hold the tension and the paradox of being human as a two-way bridge with divinity and ordinary life.

At this juncture, you are now re-calibrating your life towards a new phase of the full manifestation of the Bridge of Light; you are infusing the light of Spirit in each aspect of your daily life and reaching towards Source and the Divine to guide your life on this earth, bridging earth and stars. Bridges of Light as a method, a process, of becoming a Bridge of Golden Light… we are that! We are wholehearted, wise multidimensional beings, electrical, transformative and alive.

Ready and Free!

Myself as an Example

It took me six months of the grieving process after my mom's passing to find two important missing pieces.

I shared them briefly in chapter one. As a small

child, the guardian angel prayer that established a platform of spiritual life for all my unfolding journey on earth where I needed to know that I would be always guided and protected and that I was a child of the light... the Frequencies of Golden Light started there, as a dear guardian angel I encountered and developed with different breakthroughs, energy experiences, encounters, revelations in different periods of my life, never interrupting the flow of connection.

Always a Bridge of Light from the very beginning! So dearly loved and appreciated, and with a clear purpose to bridge the light of divinity into this earthly reality, world, and bridge the light with all the other co-creators in this planet. A multidimensional experience from the very start. In love with life!

The other piece I needed was the adolescent walk into the light, the bright Sun bridging into my heart to take me forward in life, where I took the courage as a warrior of the light to jump into the flow of the river of life!

Another important piece is Mom's recent transitioning into the light. I accompanied her, and she reassured me that she was well and brilliantly looking upon me with gentle, loving eyes... protecting and guiding me to the safe harbors of life like the Universal Mother, so I can have a magnificent life! That was the deal with her from the beginning, and throughout all my life with her until the very last moment in this lifetime... to be continued in the afterlife.

We closed well, in love, in peace, in glory!

She went well: when she wanted, how she wanted,

and I facilitated the process. A job well done!

Now my life is mine, I AM free. I have a wonderful platform to enjoy my life, live well and contribute my legacy profusely in service and delight for living. Thank You, Mom!

And the Frequencies of Golden Light say:

We are here for you, to help you hear her guidance as the Universal Mother... You are guided and protected always. Full Circle!

Yes! All is Real! The voice... the light... the advice... the presence... the re-adjusting that lasted 2 years... the efficiency... the close and quick departure... the continuous resolution, so swift and proper... the connections and disconnections of family and friends and my new life... All is true. All is well.

The right timing also for the book... you now are ready to wrap it all up and put it together in a coherent and luminous way, and she (Mom) is helping you indeed! You are very dearly held in your home and life, so you can proceed and go on. In joy and free and easy style... you are done... you have arrived! This is it: Calibration–Celebration! Bless your life! All is well! The Bridge of Light is brighter that ever! You are glowing!

Beautiful as a queen with a quartz crown indeed!

New revelations dawning on me...

I am the Cosmos
Having a human experience

And the Cosmos trusts me and loves me
To be the conduit available into this world
To know more of itself and contribute divine
light through me
A magnificent Bridge of Golden Light
That shines greatly
With the frequencies of higher dimensions
Where the glimmering and tingling of crystalline
liquid light forms
And pours into this vehicle
Allowing the divine to unfold

There has been a refinement of my multidimensional selves, many timelines unfolding simultaneously. The opening of a new Bridge of Golden Light with Mom is still unfolding…

So as much as all of this is happening simultaneously, there is a linearity in our daily routines that needs to be taken care of to accomplish specific tasks; the interweaving of all dimensional timelines is taking place more and more as a three-dimensional model…

Dimensions interweaving without time or space, without lines… increasingly as a cosmic oven cooking the outcomes. Interweaving dimensions are these new Bridges of Golden Light at the soul levels. New adventures, indeed! And we continue growing spiritually.

Bridging Dimensions

Communicating higher truths into everyday language, being the bridge… It is a co-creation process.

Using the bridge as dialogue, you become the Universal Human and bring that knowledge into daily life from the light, in the light, for the light.

In relational experiences, you learn to make Bridges of Light as building blocks from your independence towards others independence to be able to create healthy interdependence. Light and dark chords of our most close archetypical relationships play out in this plane and challenge us to access our expansiveness, our multidimensionality, our soul qualities for an awakening of humanity with intergalactic intelligence for energetic exchanges to happen for the greater good of all involved.

As a Bridge of Golden Light, I have always been a shining light, showering it onto very dark, twisted, situations and hard revelations—generally sessions with clients, in which they choose to grow... or not. In real life, things are either solved or not, depending on the willingness of recognizing what is.

Life Anew in the Context of What Is

This is my life: radical acceptance and gratitude for what is, and the possibility it offers to be more of my divinity here and now. As a Bridge of Light, I accept my family ties and my history as something that has marked many of my actions; now, after my mother's passing, I am able to honor my relationship with her and at the same time live a liberation process, diving deeply, honoring the sacredness of life.

I cherish the relationships that support me and

establish healthy boundaries of giving and receiving, responding to the call to keep doing the energy work that I love, enjoying my participation in the Mystery School and writing this book that is going to open so many doors in the continuous process of building ever-new and expansive Bridges of Golden Light in our multidimensional development.

I continue to be of the world, enjoying the richness of contributing, relating, discovering new ways to serve and, at the same time, learning to love myself more and live from a relaxed state of being, of knowing, of trust in a good life, in freedom and love of what is here and now for me in service of a greater good.

I know what there is to do, I can follow and trust, flow with it. Yes, like the river that I have so often noticed and felt sometimes like water waking me up, others like landing on a huge rock in the middle of the river just watching it flow by, or climbing stairs into the clouds into the angel realms and back, sometimes like radical cleansings, water still flowing and, when on the edge of a huge fall, cascading on, indeed!

CHAPTER THREE:

The Blending

——

Sitting in the comfort of my cozy apartment I feel extremely happy and nurtured by my environment. I have an expansive feeling of infinite gratitude and joy for my life and how I arrived here, to this moment.

There is heavenly music, a candle, my ceramic sculpture of the two-headed dragon—a very old guide and unseen friend that reminds me of higher flights and also the necessary grounding and the proverbial yin-yang of masculine and feminine energies swirling around.

There are green plants, natural, growing in beautiful ceramic pots that I designed and produced in my life as a ceramist. Plenty and more special objects that remind me of the multiple travels, journeys and personalities of my trajectory in this world.

Friends, characters, feelings and emotions, memories that intermingle in a space-container called home that embraces me and allows me to be carried away through different portals into multiple dimensions, none of this world.

I now consider myself a Bridge of Light. If everything is energy and we are clusters of vibration and frequencies establishing resonance with other clusters of vibration, I want to share the experience of my Unique Self in dialogue with the Universe and back, meaning the Universe speaking through me as me.

This is one coordinate of the equation of being in a human body connected to this amplified field of consciousness. Bridging back and forth to express and manifest this connection in this 3D world called my "ordinary life." By the way, no place better to create my reality than home.

There are the other coordinates, though: the horizontal interaction in this world with my fellow humans and the natural environment that are part of the co-creation formula to build Bridges of Light also. We will go more into that in the chapter about The Relationships further on.

So yes: bridges, paths, connections, experience, a stream of awareness that make up my life as a Bridge of Light. This is what this book is about, the sharing of multidimensional experiences in my ordinary life in the hope that others confirm and discover that there is much more than meets the eye, that we are much more and there are infinite possibilities of co-creation individually, collectively and globally when we expand our consciousness and allow the Universe to flow through us as us. Only then we will be able to create a new world of love, compassion, peace and beauty where we can all abide with a new set of rules of golden hearts, bringing heaven to earth, bridging dimensions, bridging realities, bridging the light as gifts of Grace for all of humanity.

The splendor is unbearable.

Bridges of Light is a poetic expression of bridging the light. There is no here or there in the light. There are shades of light in a dual world in which we live, and we can see the light because there is also darkness… the absence of light.

So, actually, we are talking about illuminating your world. Bringing, bridging more light to each situation and as we ourselves are made of that light we enhance and expand ourselves more when we bring, bridge, open to more light into our lives and between each other. We are then building Bridges of Light.

It resembles the lattice theory of quantum physics, which actually has been the modality of energy work calibrating the electromagnetic field of the human body, that I have been practicing, teaching and developing for more than 20 years now and became my way of life and my experience of the world. It allowed me to understand myself as a Cosmic Being living a human life.

Life Experience

I am undergoing a transition to the new me, the higher octave that the world now needs. It stems from my joy of living and expanding my consciousness as a really sacred and important purpose that stemmed from the first time I stepped out of my family environment to go to Europe. There, I met some interesting people and changed direction: from a scientific interest to a humanist context that made me leave my parents' home and dive into my life's journey as a social activist, working with prisoners, peasants, rural communities and poor people. I bridged with government programs using fun methods such as popular theater... bridging the light.

With the solid foundation of Zen Buddhism, I eventually became leader of Casa Zen in Mexico City. Then, I jumped from there to the channeling world, meeting Peggy Phoenix Dubro and the EMF Balancing Technique®. I dedicated my life to living energetically aware and bridging the light with many other teachers and schools of conscious evolution.

Stepping forward as a Bridge of Light, I made my first website, continuing the work giving EMF sessions and trainings and expanding my body of work landing in the Mystery School. I began writing spiritual poetry, along with daily meditation practice, integrating all of my experience.

After the workshop of awakening to a new paradigm, the call to write this book reinforced by my clearer connection with the Light Frequencies with which I communicate daily, now with a clearer resonance after journaling for more than 15 years. The blending is present in my writing and in my life. I trust the process, I live from there and express it in my worldly life and I am always guided in every moment, even if I do not feel it, even if I forget and let my ego surface when it was already dissolved. Humbly, I address it and do my Shadow Work or my inner child work, which reminds me to love myself dearly, appreciate the experience that is, embrace it and allow the process. I always come out the other side wiser and more loving towards myself and others, until the next time.

Lifetimes

I am aware that my soul is eternal. Now, I am further opening up to my development of the soul as a layered experience towards the Divine to bring more of my divinity into my daily life. My past and lifetimes and identities intertwine, creating and nourishing what I am today.

My Buddhas, my Divine Dragon of the Light and my ceramic pots remind me of other lifetimes.

I was a Tibetan Zen monk in the "cellars," with access to thousands of sacred books written in Sanskrit and chanting with mesmerizing Tibetan bowls that with heavenly sounds brought us all in a collective dream of expanded consciousness, where we could telepathically communicate in the multiple hours of silent practice we held together, sitting in meditation.

I have found bits and pieces of that lifetime in this one. I found myself doing lots of "sesshins" in the Rochester Zen Center with Roshi Philippe Kapleau, who brought the Zen tradition of Soto-Rinzai Zen from Japan to America. I communicated with a stone Buddha sculpture in the patio of the Center and also with Kanzeon in an intimate room. He was the same one that was a deity in India, later in China Kuan Yin and Avalokiteshvara in India. I even did the chants and the flower arrangements, ikebana style, at Casa Zen in Mexico City, where I did my practice and even became a leader for some years named by Sensei, Roshi's Dharma heir.

Many lifetimes to recall, indeed! In another, I was a ceramist in Japan. There I was also a monk, the elegance and sobriety of the Japanese style crossed dimensions and was brought over in the beautiful ceramic pots I produced years ago and have now in my living room.

The dragon—my two-headed dragon sculpture on a table in the middle of my living room—reminds me of a lifetime in China during which I was also a warrior, then a samurai in Japan... an imperial dragon that represents "wisdom" for the Chinese and whose main characteristic is having 5-fingered paws, as mine does.

It is on this same dragon that I emerged after I hit the bottom of the deep ocean: I mounted it and flew away.

This event transcended a repeating nightmare that I had when I was a child: I woke up repeatedly with a sense of drowning, being swallowed by a huge wave as the mouth of the dragon... over and over...

The event consisted of a one-hour meditation, after which I went to sleep and dreamed of the dive into the deep ocean; the darkness was illumined by the light of small fish as I hit the bottom. Then came the impulse upwards, emerging with a force that brought me out on the back of my forever Divine Dragon of the Light.

For years in my dreams I was told to make a sculpture, which I did: a two-headed dragon with a yin-yang center, the masculine and feminine forces of the Universe intertwined. When he saw it, Sensei sanctioned it as an exquisite Chinese sculpture and was very surprised when I told him the story of how I made it.

So… bits and pieces of my lifetimes in China and Japan—and more, I believe, in the eastern cultures—I have found in this one, where for years I have been related to Zen now revisiting.

As a ceramist discovering the mysteries of the four elements combined, earth, air, water and fire allowed me to create and make these beautiful ceramic pieces that bring with them the story of the ages, the elegance of Spirit, the presence of the forces of nature expressed in delicate sophisticated ways to elevate our human spirit and to remind us that there is much more soul in them that meets the eye.

I am cradled in the warmth of the infinite lifetimes that show up the minute I take the entryway and sit and let the Universe meditate me.

Then affirmations and prayers stay with me for cycles of time to serve my growth and spiritual development:

Divine Dragon of the Light
Please protect me from negativity
Inspire and help me know what I want,

Accept what I know
Do what I can
With Joy, Love, Ecstasy, Abundance, Enthusiasm,
Peace, Harmony and Lightness
For Myself and all sentient beings,
So be it!

Or the following:

My existence has a purpose
I live, I love
I work, I die
I feel refreshed and
I begin my life anew

These became daily mantras mapping my orientation in life:

Divine Love Source
Cosmic energy
Universal Love
Help me have no self-pity
No self-delusion
Utter severance with the little ego
Time effort, patience, perseverance and courage
Honesty, will power, love, understanding, truth
Walk the path of my spiritual growth.
So be it!

As of now, the ancestor of Kwan Yin is Avalok-iteshvara in India, and Cascade, the guiding feminine character, is a representation in me of the Goddess's lineage. This lineage is present in my current life: as a social activist, studying sociology at the university, I could not wait to do my social service in the male prison, where I used popular theater as an educational tool for three years. I showed up to the prison twice a week, being a very young woman... I don't know what I was thinking! But I learned a lot.

I became for the prisoners an iconic figure. For some I was a confidant, for others the idealization of a female figure that allowed them to fantasize about possibilities in their own lives with female friends. I learned about my own prisons, the ones that had to do with the paradigm we live in and the conditioning of family, community, religion and culture as a child of immigrants that came from Italy to build a life in a far and very foreign country not well known in Europe at the time: Mexico, a magical and exotic country full of contradictions, social inequality and poverty, but also brimming with genius, ingenuity, family values and cultural traditions linked to medicine men and women, some of them great shamans immersed in a sea of old energy dynamics and traditional wisdom.

Popocatépetl (Mexican Volcano)

The beautiful, monumental nature brought me once to the base of the iconic Popocatépetl volcano near a river of pristine waters and luscious plants in a jungle environment to an interesting, sacred experience with hallucinogenic mushrooms that shook my very foundations:

> *The house was burning... I saw it consumed by the flames. I looked at the chasm, a massive, dark throat... I was standing there on the edge... I saw the night sky, full of stars... I danced with drums, felt the pulse of the earth, I was mesmerized by a tree... a bridge between heaven and earth... roots running deep and in unison, its heart and mine beating as one... Born of the stars and of the earth, as if I had just landed from distant galaxies and found myself awakening into this human body. Roots run deep.*

I thought of Siddhartha when he was meditating by the river and so I refreshed my eyes with the cold water of melted snow coming from higher realms. That woke me up completely.

Another remembrance rose up:

Wild strawberries in the fields reminded me of the song we sang when I was a child, picking strawberries in the woods:

Noi siamo le fate del bosco, tra li la li la ("We are the fairies of the woods")

Noi siamo le streghe del bosco, tra li la li la ("We are the witches of the woods")

Le streghe e le fate (the fairies and the witches) co-living in the stories of a fantasy tale made up by real characters that unfolded in the trajectory of a lifetime on earth.

This is the journey about how we become endeared

after landing from distant worlds in this beautiful, luscious planet that has become home... for now, our only home in the known universe.

We came down the mountain, guided by a medicine man that told of the story and healing properties of all kinds of plants and bushes on our way back to "civilization."

Egypt (An Experience in This Lifetime)

I hear the drumbeats of my heart and I am in Egypt, about to enter the queen's pyramid in the desert or Cairo. I just found a shell in the sand that reminds me of the changing of the ages, as this desert was once the bottom of the ocean.

Today, we can see these enormous pyramids, built eons ago and surely with the help of more evolved beings form other worlds.

There is memory in each of the blocks of stone, and you can tune into it each step of the way into the pyramid. As I was going to embark into a deep dive into the pyramid with other fellow humans crossing the underworld I prepared. There are myths of protecting yourself from the dark forces that lurk around when you enter.

So I squat inside, following a queue of people going up the tunnel, and suddenly I fell into a dark abyss of forgetfulness. I fainted. The person in front of me pulled me and the one in the back pushed me. They could not afford to stop the flowing of the queue in the middle of a tunnel where you could not even stand up fully and you needed to advance hunkering down.

At the end of the tunnel I was awake again and found myself in the queen's room in the center of the pyramid... no hieroglyphs or colors, only a black marble sarcophagus.

People stood around me in a circle that formed itself naturally as they were entering the chamber... I am at the center, radiating brilliant bluish light that feels liquid, the boundaries between my inner organs disappearing... I am speaking words that come through me from another dimension... my heart is pounding...

People in the circle listening and watching me had visions of Mother Mary... of a rainbow... everything stopped for a few minutes... inundated by the light... all in silence... revelations happened... I was still in a trance-like state... when I restarted walking to leave the chamber.

Then the queue continued flowing, and we hunkered down and continued along the same tunnel through which we had entered.

What happened here?

An entryway to a space of no time where karmic patterns untangle, awakening unfolds and the wisdom of the ages swirls around as spirals of light that come and go from the deepest corners the Cosmos... and I was a beacon of light for a few seconds when all could see beyond limitations, as in a dream that you can forget... or as a real event that you vividly remember after many years, an experience that now, with a wiser perception, you can understand as a crossing of dimensions.

As multidimensional beings that we are there are Bridges of Light with other dimensions going on all the time, there are synchronicities that if we pay attention take us into other dimensions that cannot be measured with our human linearity or time clocks. The revelations, visions, breakthroughs we have are pieces of the puzzle that we need to live a more integrated and fuller life in this lifetime. We will talk more about this in the next chapter where we address multidimensionality as a cosmic being having a human experience.

It took some time to integrate this experience. For a while I could not fully come back into my body... I shook and cried very often and needed help to assimilate and be able to function in my daily life.

It is in this process of validating my own experience and interpreting it to learn the lessons that it brought to me where you are allowing your life to change through the whispers of the soul. Here is where for me the journaling has always had a predominant role to play in not only the recording of the experience but in the unfolding dialogue with my unseen friends that is in itself a profound contemplation of our multidimensionality and interconnectedness not only in an horizontal plane with all of our other co-creators, but also in the development of our spiritual life and our expansion of consciousness.

It looks as if there were unfinished themes that cross over between lifetimes and remain unresolved, reproducing themselves across generations, karmic knots that start to get untangled when you let them. My energy work in this lifetime and all the meditation that I have done and continue to do are great tools for just that: for them to unfold and finally dissolve, bringing healing and an openness that allows more light to finally come in.

It feels like jumping into portals, there are worlds of concentric circles that appear when awareness is aware of itself. There are glimpses as shining streaks of light call to you and you hear whispers of the soul in the distance coming closer, like a breeze reminding you of other times, other spaces, other voices. So many worlds.

The Worlds

Inspired by the guided meditations
I am alive, I am electrical, I am awake
The worlds exist in me
I am the world, I am in the world,
We are co-creators of worlds
We are ONE
I play
I experience a continuum going in and out
The eyelids are just a veil between dimensions
The objects are alive and magic occurs
Bridges between the worlds
I re-decorate my spaces and discover new dimensions
My multidimensionality expands

The journey into Infinite Possibilities is
delicious!
There are no limits
Bewildered! When there is no world there is only
emptiness
It all starts with the fullness in my heart
The worlds exists inside of me
I open my eyes and I see the painting
It is a reminder of those worlds
The heart is whole and lives in between the sun
and the moon
It wakes up creating worlds of conscious
innovation
It allows effective reality building
I live knowing that the world does not exist
without my experience of it
I am not separate, the world starts inside
I co-create my most enlightened life
I find my way into reality as an evolutionary
emerging
Expressing everyday as a bridge of light
And so it is!

Crossing the portal, the gates open and the journey
into the unknown continues with a familiar feeling,
as your path is unique in the ocean of consciousness.
Stars appear, the spaciousness is there, the joy and the
celebration are just beginning even if you know they
have always been there.

Each time we remember who we are, the cells of
the body vibrate with joy. Thus, the layers of my DNA

rejoice and the fibers of light of my being dance, generating rainbows of shades of light in the spaciousness, arousing feelings of pleasure in my body.

I discover intelligences that live within. There is the core spiritual intelligence, the intelligence of the heart, the one that radiates in the plexus and even that of the guts. All of them are energies that meld into the galaxies that opened up when you open the gates.

There are corners of the soul I revisit. There is a very early one that started when I was driving in a very populated avenue in Mexico City... suddenly, I was above the traffic in a web of light, a defined tapestry that took me to an elevator. I rose to another level of consciousness in tube of electric blue light. I stepped out and I found myself in a luscious, wonderful greenery: plants, flowers, tall grass with crystals and diamonds laying around vibrating.

I hear the sound of water falling and approach, finding the Cascade. I step into the huge pool and enter the Cascade, which cleanses my soul of all the dust of the ages and refreshes my spirit. Nearby, to the left, there has always been a huge dome of light, and I go inside...

There are many beings of light weaving strings and fibers of light, waving their hands and performing exquisite movements to heal the souls. There are golden and platinum energies melding around and celestial crystalline sounds.

No wonder I love to do energy sessions: this is where I go when I do that.

The lotus flower is present too. Its core has a

pinkish hue and it is constantly flowering and opening up; there is a stream of energy that comes out from the heart of the Universal human all the time and nurtures the tapestry of colors and sounds in the healing dome where miracles happen.

There is also another level, underground. I go down and meet with a sleeping trickster: he has to do with the Shadow World, with cosmic jokes and humor, appearing as magic tricks when he jumps into the caves of being.

I can rest in the arms of the Dharma knowing I am loved and protected and I relax in the womb of Infinite Self until the next time.

The Connection with the Ocean

In the horizon, you see a line where the water meets the sky. Leaning forward, you perceive the rotation of the earth. You fall into the arms of a brilliant sun, the oblique rays on the surface of the ocean are a golden sparkling carpet that mesmerizes the soul.

You dive in with us and we meld... blend... Frequencies of Golden Light...

The hot tea warms me also... there is a blending with the warm water that soothes the soul, and we become so intimate... because that is what I do with the Frequencies of Golden Light. It's not channeling: it is a blending. This is also what happens with my spiritual poetry: I blend listening to the frequencies with my own automatic writing, and thus they flow.

You need to go on with the book, with us, now. We will continue to build the intimacy together... there has been a distinction between your Higher Self and us, the Frequencies of Golden Light for the clarity of our communication and a definite reminder of the love, the unconditional love, that you feel is from your Higher Self and us. How intimate we are. Time to create together, time to enjoy the building blocks for an extraordinary joyful and playful ground of being. You are ready to rejoice in the flow of life and celebrate the miracle of being alive and be a human in this auspicious time. Life is enough indeed!

We are already blended, as you are the Bridge of Light, a conduit for us to be with you. So you are with us. This is what it means when you affirm "I am with the Bridges of Golden Light:" you and we together are those bridges. We are blended!

Your Higher Self is the Bridge of Light. Your mundane Self is the container of all of it, as the body is multidimensional too. Generally felt as changes of temperature in the body, the warmer, more golden energies and the platinum, cooler energies. All your knowing of this helps in our communication. We are very grateful for you receiving us! Thank you! Much love!

The Marvel of Life

Yes, the expansion!
The miracle of breathing
The expansion and contraction of the Universe
Where we can float forever in awe of life
Just sitting!
What a mystery revealing itself

Penetrating the layers of what is
Finding a simple truth at the very bottom
We are alive!
And this is the ultimate mystery
The joy and privilege to be human
The expansion of consciousness happens
With the universe manifesting through us
In unique ways
No need to limit those expressions with the
mind
We are meditated by divinity itself
It expands with each conscious breath
Illuminating the whole Cosmos
What a privilege to be alive forever!
As the coming and going of the ocean waves it
never stops
As the movement of the stars and planets and
galaxies
With all of the laws of nature continue the cos-
mic dance of the eons and eons Of the coming
and goings
What a marvel life is… indeed!

In my experience, I am in control of my life. I can let go of myself in the sea of consciousness, there is a unique presence that is me, very intimate with the Universe. The expression of divinity through me is what I want to express fully in my daily life. My presence brings out the truth in others, there is a quality of integrity that cannot be avoided. Honesty is a vibrant frequency. The blending is the experience, and I hold the tension!

I have always been free, from the very beginning. The rebel in me never indulged the requirements of any specific society. My life has been adventurous, creative, productive and free, and it has served as a lighthouse, helping many people.

There was a book I wrote in August 1987 called *Arco iris* ("rainbow" in Spanish). Its illustrated chapters, in the form of a play (I was doing popular theater at the time), covered various educational topics. 10,000 copies were made for an audience of rural cultural promoters working in the country's poorest communities.

Girasol (a play on words, as in Spanish it means "sunflower" but also, in a more literal way, "spin the sun") was a project for a cultural healing center. Even if it did not fully materialize, it represented more than 5 years of great service for a community of growing souls who at the time needed support.

There was always work towards the light, always guided and the antecedents for my later energy work as the foundation of a lifestyle of service, and creative endeavors.

Life Is All There Is

Flowing, joyfully carried by the river of life really... I love the little waves, the whirlpools that seem to swallow it all up or smaller ones that pull together leaves and sticks to organize a spiral. The rock in the middle of the river that I reached by jumping over smaller ones. I sit there, letting the sunlight warm me and mesmerize me with the reflections in the water.

This is always a bridge for me into other dimensions of light. The spectrum of light is huge and the bandwidth of colors and emotions that go with it tells me that emotion is energy in motion.

We can live in the space of no space between dimensions, just rest for a while in some of them or explore the reality of one realm. There are always these bridges from one to another that interface and draw the map of each journey into the unknown realm of the soul that is vast and glorious, where I can rest when I am tired of the business of life and talk with the angels that caress my hair and reassure me that all is well in the universe.

And so it is!

Life is really simple when your trust lies in the divine. I step into it. It is a posture: a core posture, in which you first smile at yourself and your humanness and then stare into the void; in the silence, some movement starts and you wait in the sacred space.

If you are able to go through life like this, as the sacred silence, you can really flow into the cracks of it and discover a small blooming flower in dialogue with a twinkling little star and remember that we are born from the earth as well as from the stars.

Keep it simple, low and vast with deep breaths, sighs that bring the whispers of the soul. You can hear them if you listen and allow the breeze to caress your face and the blending to do its magic.

It is really as if I could touch the space between the atoms, knowing that the vibration will call the next experience and the next. Tranquility and freedom are possible.

It is good that there is a table, the kitchen table where we can sit, talk, have coffee, cry and laugh with another or others, and we are always touching the edges of the infinite in a smile or even with words. When we allow the cracks to become translucent. Life is all there is.

CHAPTER FOUR:

The Relationships

———

The river of relationships, the interweaving of all the shades of light… as we live in a relational world where everything is relationship, not only with other fellow human beings as co-creators but with all of the natural world, the material world and, of course, the multidimensional worlds… all this makes up the multicolored tapestry of life.

The Beginning

I could see the cell splitting in two
Those two splitting in four
The myriad forms of the process of creation
There were millions of grains of sand and water
The horizon, the longing, forward and backwards, up and down,
The integration started to vanish
Separation was frightening
It was I splitting into myriad forms as a Big Bang

The tranquility and the darkness of the Womb of
the Infinite Self shattered
Inward and Outward
Stars and Universes
In the middle of the hurricane
There was water
Light and Dark

I left my parents' home when I was 18, after finishing high school. The rebel in me that had decided
to study a scientific career decided that I first needed
to break out of the family circle, so I went to Europe
with a friend. It was my first time away from home. I
met a new world, and my circle of relationships grew
in such a way that when I came back from the "Old
World" I was a different person. My interest for science was not a priority anymore, and the humanistic
perspective of life took first place. Many questions,
reflections, contemplations and the search for those
answers drove me to numerous adventures.

I needed the freedom to explore, so I left my parents' home early for the standards of Mexico's Catho-
lic, conservative society. Those standards were exacerbated by my family history: my parents were Italian
immigrants who never fully assimilated into their new
world and carried with them the traumas of war. My
grandfather fought in both World Wars and my father
found himself facing the firing squad twice during
World War II, about to be executed first by Tito's sup-
porters and then by the Germans. On both occasions,
he saved himself by offering his translation services,

having been born of a German mother and an Italian father who died at a very young age. His identity issues were evident all through his life and left him deep scars that were not his fault but the result of the age in which he was born, where human beings killed each other over nationalities. Sadly, this absurd and evil behavior persists to this day.

Considerations About Our Human Story

Abandonment sucks!
If the light shines on an object that has its own identity, that produces the shadow
The shadow is not a dump or a trash can, it is not evil or darkness
We made it that!
The light-God has always shined on us, and our unique and multidimensional shadows are only an expansion of God
Actually our myriad forms are God expanding and experimenting itself
Like an old movie projector
Imagine: the bulb is God, the film is you
Projecting on a screen all the shades of light that show myriad stories
Collective consciousness is all of the infinite movies together
If God has always shined its light on me
I could go and live all the lives and adventures I wanted
Lifetime after lifetime
I misinterpreted all along that I was abandoned

It had to do with an original misunderstanding
Programming me into the "abandonment sucks"
statement of living
Reprogramming
If I am the producer of the films
I am also the projector and I am also the bulb
Isn't this my Universal Calibration Lattice?
My Core Energy radiating unto the Cosmic
Lattice?
Interconnected both, in resonant communication
I have been producing and projecting movies all
the time
Now, imagine more
The projector-light-bulb-God-me
In the center projecting movies over spherical
screen all around me
Editing the little frames of the film in a circular
spherical fashion of Now time
All the shades of light as colors and stories mani-
festing right before my very eyes Created me!
I am God also…
Now, just looping and listening!
Enjoying the playground of Creation
Expanding God…
Calibration—Celebration!

Just this morning I edited all of the movies of my childhood that my father did and that we watched with that old movie projector… He is having a ball!

After 4 months in Europe, I no longer fit into the little familiar circle I had left behind to start a journey far beyond what I had imagined.

When I was 13 years old, I had a life-shaping experience. My father could not stand me been on the phone with my friends all the time, having my nails painted red and a lot of other aspects of my teenage personality for which he constantly judged and punished me gravely. This one time, he called me names without reason and told me I would need to leave the household and go live somewhere else.

I went to my room. I did not cry: I had developed the habit of not doing so due to the beatings I received from my neurotic mother when I did; I held it in to prove my strength, in my view. At that moment, I decided that it was totally unfair to tell a thirteen-year-old who could not support herself to go live somewhere else. I concluded that he was saying it only to hurt me and show his power over me. I made a promise to myself: as soon as I was grown up and could support myself, I would leave my parents' home.

I never forgot the promise I made to myself. When I returned from Europe, it took a year for me to get a job and the means to get the hell out of there. I stormed out, shouting at my dad that he was a terrible capitalist and that I was leaving to help the revolution of the poorest of the poor in a country whose inequalities broke my heart.

The Morning After

What a release!
Such freedom from the constraint

I can understand now how unique I am
In and from the Womb of Infinite Self
All of new creation is possible
Infinite possibilities
Because I own me
And I am God also…
That lost and hidden part of me
It's me also…
I love my Shadow Self!
There is nothing and nobody
That can tell me how things are
It is only experience
My experience!
My absolute experience
Unique experience
No restrictions—No obligations
Peace—Being at peace
Nowhere to go
Nothing to do
Only to feel perfectly and totally alive!
All the senses awakened
Expansion definitively comes from within
I can be the Observer and the Creator at the
same time
Relaxation from Expectations!
It feels so good…

So my life away from home continued. I became a seeker of truth, my truth—reflection and contemplation, accompanied by my journaling, which has always been my dialogue with my Higher Self and all the other beings of light, angels, shamans in seen and unseen realms that always partnered with me in my journeys into the unknown. I have a long list of records in my journals.

One of the first tools I needed to process my life after some years away from home and with plenty of adventures to tell was psychoanalysis, which at the time provided an important introspective method. I started with about 3 years of individual psychoanalysis and then 2 years in a group. This was my first round; later on, after some deep relationship crises, I had another long round of individual sessions.

The first round ended when my psychoanalyst told me that I needed to... kill my inner child! He said she was giving me so much trouble and was too much of a rebel. I guess he did not like that I brought some dope into a group session to make us all relax and enjoy the tense and intense moments we were going through. I never forgave him for that. One cannot pretend to be as liberal and open as he was and then be outraged by a simple act of innocence to the point of saying such a monstrosity!

Instead, I learned to take care of her. When she cries, I hug her; when she screams, I calm her down; when she needs to unwind, I take her to the movies; when it is time for me to play, I call her in first. She is invited and is allowed to do whatever she wants in that spirit of playfulness. I taught her how to speak, how to stand up for herself and how to be a beacon of light in the world for herself and others, the weakest of the weak who could not speak for themselves.

For someone who was always told to shut up, to be proper, to not speak or laugh so loudly when I was just a little girl, it was too much. But my rebellious spirit never ever quit or succumbed to the tyranny of the dictators. That's probably why I have had so many issues with authority and have always confronted and challenged them, as David did with Goliath.

My younger me did popular theater in prison as a sociologist. It was a way of reminding the prisoners that they could dream their life out of there, that the Spirit was so much broader and that beyond the constraints of the mind there were ample, colorful worlds. I learned to recognize my own prison and with our work together we liberated the Spirit and re-learned to dream and play!

My inner child is very much alive to this day. It is refreshing to find her so alive and well in these confined, restricted, oppressive, turbulent times. I live well with her and she has learned to live with me. We truly, authentically love each other dearly and this is what allowed me to care for my aging mother, difficult and dominant as she was, in a playful way. A paradox indeed!

If there is any good advice you can take from this book, it is to love your inner child divinely, as she/he is divine!

Shadow Self

Looking at the darker clouds in the sky

I could appreciate more the brightness of the
light
Because of the existing darker clouds
The contrast made it possible to appreciate the
multicolored layer
Of the shades of light
My Shadow Self is the possibility to appreciate
The brightness of my Infinite Self
With all the different shades of light
That I would not be able to appreciate in its
entire splendor
If there were only light!

From Cosmic Consciousness

I must share that in the middle of writing this book I got sick. Very sick. I got Covid—for three years I had been able to avoid it and now I got it, almost a year after my mother passed away and in the middle of selling her apartment (which she left to both me and my sister). Although vaccinated, the weakness it causes—among many other symptoms—is unbearable. It has been almost two weeks and I am almost normal; the digestive issues, the weariness, the depression that came over me are starting to loosen their grip on me.

I could not write during this period, and just then the relationship topic really reached its top crisis… how was I going to write about them if everything was crumbling down big time, starting with my relationship with myself and the Divine in me?

I was in a workshop with one of The Mystery School teachers, working through the issues of communication and committing to what is. I experienced disastrous feelings as my worst fears came up:

I am terrified of remaining completely alone.

I feel I am broken, incapable of loving or being loved.

I feel like a failure in my energy work. I have no clients.

I was hitting rock bottom on all fronts. The raw truth is that I am in transition… big time.

Suddenly, I realize that it was the Universe, as always, testing me to see if I really am the Bridge of Light I claim to be—first and foremost to myself. I decided I was going to take the test indeed!

Next, I joined a four-day spiritual retreat with Jeff Carreira in the Mystery School called Resting in Cosmic Consciousness and… guess what? I am doing just that. After one day of silent meditation as the Cosmos experiencing its human form, I've noticed far fewer thoughts than usual. I experience a clean slate, and I feel lighter and more expanded. I realize that I am actualizing the Bridge of Light I am building in this moment. A new one in my sequel of Bridges of Light method that happens with the processes I follow in my own spiritual evolution.

One with the Divine

I Cosmos having a human experience
Cosmos meditates in gratefulness of what is
All that transpired is what is given by the divine

I love the little one that has endured
I love the big one that lives through me
We are the greatest team there is
We expand the love of light as a bridge of the
light of the Cosmos into this world
What moves me back and forth is the bridge of
light
I love the Divine
The Divine loves me
We are One in love
I rest in cosmic consciousness in gratitude and
love
I am open to receive the blessings bestowed,
I am available
I know I will be taken care of
Deeply in love with the sacred
I am in total surrender
Burning in passion for the Divine

My Father

We loved each other dearly, but it was nowhere near an easy relationship. Since I was very young, my soul decided that she wanted to save him. I decided I was going to rescue him.

He was the best of fathers when my sister and I were little. Always present and caring, joyful and happy to be with us.

But then I lost him. I was nine years old, and my parents and grandparents took a trip together by car from Mexico City to the United States when the irreparable happened.

A drunken man came speeding out of the blue, driving against traffic, as my father drove past another car. In the front-to-front collision, the man died and all the occupants of the car—my parents and my grandparents—suffered severe injuries and broken bones. They were taken in by the police authorities and my father spent years signing papers and reiterating his innocence on bail every month.

He came back defeated and depressed, a changed man. He was never the same joyful presence again: he felt guilty and responsible forever. He had served in World War II when he was very young, he had faced German and Italian firing squads in a divided world where his identity was tested to the bone, and now this happened as he was the a father of 2 little girls in a foreign country… he never got over it, and his depressive shadow took over. He had emphysema and other dysfunctions, but I can say that when he died, the life-long depression exacerbated by that fateful accident was a major factor.

My very young soul, loving him so much, wanted to rescue him. Later in his life and mine, having left home at a very early age (he never forgave me for that), I did: I went back to him and worked for him as an insurance agent and when he got ill, he would have lost his business if I hadn't been there to save at least two-thirds of his portfolio, allowing my mother to live well after he passed. I call this a clearing of karma.

After that, I was offered a career in the insurance world, but I declined: I had suffered a major betrayal

by my father's business partner, who had never accepted me as a fair and equal player and just wanted to
keep my father's business for himself.

It was very painful for me to discover a conspiracy
between the leaders of the industry—including my father—to eliminate me from the game. They set me
up for unpaid insurance fees of clients that were really
stolen by one of the employees to frame me. I endured
harsh treatment and even received death threats. In
the end, I solved the issue (quite brilliantly, I might
add) by selling my father's portfolio back to his business partner. That move allowed me to get out of the
bully-ridden, male-dominated world of insurance.

What hurt me the most was my father's alliance
with the conspiracy against me. He treated his partner
as the son he never had, as he had wanted me to be
a boy from the very start. Such a big blow brought
me to the next phase after some overwhelming experiences with patriarchal culture. In the world of relationships, this was my confirmation that to be an
intelligent, professional and honest woman in a male-
dominated culture would make you a target of resistance and critical judgements that did not honor new
or innovative ways of doing things.

I moved on to another chapter of my life. This one
had to do with emotional release, healing modalities,
shamanic work, energy work and a whole new world
that I was very passionate about discovering… and I
fell in love with the teacher.

I learned a lot but also paid my fees… betrayal was
once again my reward for more than 6 years of diving

deep into this relationship that ended up almost killing me. He could not stand my empowerment and wanted to keep me down. Literally. One day, as he lay over me, strangling me to shut me down, my guardian angel gave me the strength to break free and breathe again.

That started a longer period of 6 months during which I had to undo the business and the life we had created together and start from scratch by myself. I have always been a fervent student of life, and in this new age world I always studied the best tools of self-discovery, personal development, spiritual workshops and healing modalities that I first applied to myself and then practiced in service. I did a lot in that arena, you name it, and as a sponge and as a self-taught person instructed by my own means I always found the best of all the worlds.

My incursions covered a lot of ground: massage, aromatherapy, a Medical Assistance Program with flower essences, astrology, oracle cards, healing modalities like reiki and tensegrity, shamanic steam rooms, white magic works, channeling with angels, the extensive study of bridging science and spirituality with the top leaders in the field and many, many workshops and practices with the most avant-garde people in the field.

This was a lot of wisdom and practical knowledge that I integrated during the years with diligent study and practice. It gave me a good platform for what was going to come next, the topic of the next chapter: my energy work.

My Mother

From a soul perspective, this is one of the most entrenched relationships I've ever had (and continue to have). Dear angel Torah once said that the luminous and dark chords of love and hate are interwoven as serpents in a basket—precisely those that deal with mother-daughter and sister-sister relationships, and they are so intense and strong because of the love there is. I did not completely understand what he meant at the time. A good friend once said that one of the purposes of life was to go through the death of our parents. At the time, I did not understand that either.

I owed it to myself to be present when that time came… for my father 18 years ago and for my mother last year, on January 26, 2022.

My conscience is clear. I was there very present in both occasions and I realize that the completion cycle of grief takes its own time. In the case of my mother, as I said before, I am still in the middle of it… and when I review our relationship, it was intense from the very beginning.

This is the story I've told myself, the one I have lived with almost all my life. As the first child born into a loving relationship of Mom and Dad, the story is that everybody was thrilled—even though my father probably would have preferred a boy and my mother had already had a motherly experience, practically raising her younger sister who was almost like a child to her. That robbed me of my firstborn status. Then, after three months of being breastfed, that stopped:

my mother was pregnant with my sister, so she put me in the arms of Oma, my grandmother from my father's side.

My father had brought her from abroad to Mexico City to live with us. She was a German nurse and a massage therapist who raised my father practically by herself, as when my father was 5 years old his artist father passed away. My Oma suffered numerous miscarriages: my father was the only one that survived. She went through hell when my father was drafted by the military at 18 years old and fought in World War II. So, once he was settled in Mexico City and married to my mother, he brought her over from Italy as she was all alone there: she had been disowned by her noble family for eloping with my grandfather from Munich to Italy (Gorizia), where he had promised her flowering orange trees.

As I was deposited in her arms, I am sure I was influenced by all of this... we are so interconnected, and these chords of light and dark interweave heavily. In my story, Oma was my real mother: the other one abandoned me when she became pregnant with my sister, who was born a year later... just three days before my birthday.

Naturally, I was the favorite of my Oma and my father, while the little one was the favorite of my mother. She always protected her because she was the little one... so I was not only robbed of my firstborn status and of my mother as I landed in the arms of Oma, but I was in a kind of sandwich situation that felt compressed to say the least.

I grew used to being alone. I was very intelligent and got good grades at school, while my sister needed my mother's help with her homework… and got all the attention. I was rebellious and that always got a zero in behavior. The comparisons were unbearable and lasted until the end of high school. I was supposed to study biochemistry (because I was in love with my biology teacher), but then I left for Europe and things changed completely.

Away from home, my vision shifted. I saw myself from another perspective, a European one; I realized that I was perfectly okay in "the New World" (Mexico for me), that I was a humanist and that I was going to join the revolution for the poor after having met two German guys that instructed me in communism.

I am a child of the 60s. Once back from Europe and with my communist, radical views, the arguments that erupted between my father and me made life impossible for the four of us. We were all liberated when finally I left home before even turning 20. My mother later told me that she felt guilty for having been happy when I left, as she was really fed up of the fighting between my father and me. I also think it was for the best: I broke out of the very restrictive family circle that was suffocating me.

My mom tried to stay connected with me and not lose touch completely and she bought an apartment in the southern part of the city, where I had decided to live to be as far away from them as possible. Bless her soul, as it is the home I am still living in nowadays, and I do not know if I would be having a home if she hadn't given me this one.

Later on, when my sister got married and moved to the States, my mother was devastated. Her little favorite that had finally married and would give her granddaughters was gone.

I already knew I would never marry: I did not believe in marriage and I knew from very early on that I wouldn't have children of my own by choice. Later on in life, I had many students, clients and pupils, but never biological children. I was too busy with the revolution of the poor and then rebelling against the patriarchal environment in the insurance business that permeated society. My mother was not thrilled. She was very traditional, pragmatic and dominant. A master controller, she never agreed with any of the endeavors, passions and callings I had in life and pursued diligently.

A breaking point came when I discovered that my mother had appointed my sister's husband as the executor of her will. I'd had it. She'd done that to favor my sister because she was not here and I "did not have a man to take care of me." When I rebelled against this situation, my sister walked out and that was it for her. She never forgave my mother for changing the executor; we had never gotten along, but this time she cast me out of her life for good. She kept coming between my mother and me, saying I was living at her expense (which I wasn't); she didn't want the money my mother gave me to affect her half of the inheritance, so she resorted to constant emotional blackmail.

My mother was held hostage by the manipulation

of my sister, who regarded money as her god. She'd sold herself to her husband's family and left me to care for our widow mother alone. Mom used to say that I would be the cane of her old age... and I was.

The difficult thing for me was that I was considered the villain all the time by my mother. I could not have a clear relationship with her because she was cruelly manipulated by my sister and, as she so often said, she would have liked me to be more like her (rather than so different in my beliefs, values, lifestyle and so on). In her opinion, I never made it in life, but even if I was a total disappointment for her, she was comforted by the fact that at least one of her daughters was there for her.

All in all, I managed to handle the horror movie pretty well. In the last 2 years of her life there was time for reconciliation, forgiveness and even appreciation and support.

It pains me that she died so suddenly, because I felt it robbed me of some more years of enjoying a relationship that had finally become good and the caring company we had learned to be for each other as I was so dedicated to taking care of her.

I am having a very hard time now as I realize that I was living much of my life through her: supporting her family, friendships, needs and comforts... and when she left I found myself living my worst nightmare: being completely alone.

I am picking up the pieces now and selling the apartment, the last piece of inheritance that will allow me to have much-appreciated financial support.

My Sister

From a Soul perspective, I know the karmic bonds with a sister are real and manifest in human life. Who knows how many lifetimes we shared… and in what fashion.

I lived a lifetime in the desert, during which we were both men and had a loving relationship that ended badly.

In this life, we are both Geminis, born only one year apart. And yet, we could not be more different. As she said: if we had been born in different families, we would not even have met, since we have nothing in common. This is her way of avoiding the unavoidable karmic connection that we share because we are sisters in this lifetime.

Yes, we were separated in life very early on: from the minute my mom got pregnant, I was pushed aside and she, the little one, became the favorite—a fact never acknowledged by my mother but confirmed by reality in each instance.

We faced a cruel family reality. After that terrible accident that my father, mother and grandparents had on the highway, not only my father was lost in depression forever, but Mom's neurosis grew and she had a very light hand to beat us for whatever reason. In her impatience and stress, she was really abusive; my sister and I learned to relate to each other in that abusive way as well. We beat each other badly and then were beaten by my mother for fighting. This cycle of abuse and violence went on for a long time: I received the last slap in the face when I was 17 years old. After that, I was already gone—first diligently preparing my departure and then actually leaving my parents' home.

When my sister was in her teenage years, she preferred to eat marihuana cakes with her friends and explore her sexuality rather than play tennis all day long at the club like I did. She entered an abusive relationship with an older man; she had left home and was living in his apartment as a kind of "slave." I'm the one who saved her: I snuck in one day while he was out, helped her pick up her stuff and took her back to my parents' house. She never acknowledged it. She convinced herself that it had been a mutual friend of ours, not I, who had been her savior.

When she finally married, she did so into a Jewish family that never really got along with my father, given his German-Italian background. I was soon discarded by her husband as an unwanted person in their family. I could not even see my nieces because he decided that I, being an unmarried and childless rebel, would not be a good influence on his daughters.

Later in life I had the opportunity to give online energy sessions once a week to one of my nieces, the younger of the two. She has had a very tough life and was in a dark hole of alcoholism, drugs and an abusive relationship. For over four years, I really helped her to come out of it. She is now happily married with a beautiful daughter of her own, she studied psychology and even if she has a certain level of bipolar disorder she manages to lead a lovely life. The help I gave her was, once again, never openly acknowledged. I was kind of paid off by going on a trip with her, as her father did not want her to come to Mexico alone (they have lived in Houston for more than 30 years). A misunderstanding happened there that was orchestrated by my sister and that was it. I was cast out from my sister's family again.

After my sister moved away and built her life in a foreign country, both she and my mother suffered being so far apart. She sometimes (infrequently) came to see Mom, and whenever she did I had to retreat. The condition was not outright explicit at first, but the deal was for me to stand back when she came and stayed at my mother's place. Her husband had said that when they visited we were not going to play happy family and that he preferred me not to be present while they were here. My mother, of course, agreed. It didn't matter that I was the one who had been taking care of her for 18 years after my father died—even if we did not live in the same house, I took it as my responsibility to watch over her, despite continuing to rebel against her idea of me being the "walking stick" for her aging process... though I ended up being exactly that. She would do anything just to see my sister. Always blackmailed by her!

Almost a year before my mother passed away, my sister came to visit and this time I was there. The two years of pandemic brought us very close, isolated together as I cared for her 24/7; she was slowly decaying and having a hard time, and I helped her all I could. My sister was furious at my mother for agreeing to help me out with a bank credit that was sinking me financially. She demanded to be given the same amount I had gotten for the bank credit, and I'd had enough—I shouted so hard that the building trembled. I set things straight and my mother finally stood up for herself and for me, saying that this was it, like it or not.

Months later, my mother decided to go visit my sister (by herself, because I was never invited) in order to meet her great-granddaughter. When she arrived, my sister said she was happy to see her but that she would never forgive her for the bank credit incident. Mom's decay was evident upon returning from that trip: she had a back pain, a broken heart and felt she was done in this lifetime. From then on, she just enjoyed the daily photos of her great-granddaughter and, in my view, she was preparing to go.

One of the reasons I was so angry when she died is that, for the first time in my life, we had just begun to get close to each other. Her quick, unexpected departure did not allow me to enjoy a few more years of that for which I always yearned: Mom's acknowledgment, appreciation and love. I am grateful that I could live that in the end, but I am devastated that it could not last a little longer. It is very difficult for me to let her go. So I mourn all that was… and was not.

I am still grieving and allowing myself to honor her with it. She really mattered to me, and is the most important and prevalent relationship in my life. And my heart is broken into a million pieces for not being able to share this with my sister, who denied me big time at the funeral saying that we were not really sisters. She continues to emphasize this by excluding me from her family in every way possible.

The sale of my mother's apartment was not only the last step in the inheritance process. It closes a life chapter. Even if she wants nothing to do with me she is my sister in this lifetime and that has karmic consequences indeed!

I know it sounds weird for me to be sad over closing the cycle with someone who has been so mean to me. The thing is, from a universal perspective, we had the opportunity to be sisters, share a life and now share memories of Mom... and it was terribly wasted. I could not have a sister, and neither could she... if we were meant to be together in this lifetime, I feel we could have made something beautiful out of it instead of the mess it turned out to be. I guess what hurts is all that could have been and was not. The opportunity of a lifetime, wasted... I really wanted to have a sister, an ally in life, and as it went so badly with her, all my life I have been searching for a sister or sisterhood outside my family circle. This ordeal has been very painful and there are repeating patterns and conditionings that need to be dissolved and integrated, and this is what I must do now... indeed!

MySelf

I hadn't had a vacation for a very long time. After getting Covid, I got so exhausted and depressed, and I recognize it as only an expression of the tiredness I have accumulated after so many years of worrying about life. About my life.

My constant dialogue with myself is always open, as it has been through the years. I arrived to a point where in my morning daily meditations I can just sit, trust and surrender to the guide I receive from Spirit into my open heart and let it bring me home. I rest in it, and from there I go into my worldly life with confidence and love for the day to unfold.

I am finally resting. This year that began with my mother's death has been kind of a sabbatical. I am still allowing myself to mourn and to acknowledge my disappointment and anger over her leaving so soon... I understand now that the "so soon" is because we had just arrived to a point in our relationship where we were in close and loving care for each other, and I had longed for that all my life.

Now I see that it was precisely because of this that she could leave promptly and in peace: she had also yearned for that. We did it, in this lifetime together. This is magnificent, and in this worldly mess I did not want to let go of that. Where she dwells now and what I touch each morning when I meditate with an open heart to receive the grace and the blessings bestowed by the divine is not of this world... that is home.

As this year closes, I am able to accept the departure of my mother, I established a beautiful daily platform for my worldly life to unfold and I am infinitely grateful for what has transpired. I can allow myself to close the year in peace and gratitude and enjoy the fruits of my life's work on the most important relationship of my life.

I don't yet know how this is going to open up new venues of being in this world, and I will let winter go by in hibernation and let spring tell its story when it arrives. In the meantime, I will rest and allow life to unfold.

Betrayals

I have a rosary of relationships in my life, and I see that whether they have been friendships, romantic relationships or work connections they have usually ended in high treason, drama, betrayal and closure.

Ever since I was very young, I used to say that I'd had many children in previous lifetimes and that in this one I would not have biological children of my own, but rather in other versions: students, clients or whatever else.

I also knew that I was not going to get properly married, as this matter called "love" needed to be experienced for real, not through papers or protocols. I have always loved my sexuality and know it is sacred and has no container in boxes or labels. My relationships were one-on-one, close, honest, authentic, raw, intense. My passion for sharing my own truth with the other and discover theirs really absorbed me for the time that the relationship lasted. I tend to idealize the object of my love, and when life unfolds everything generally crumbles down.

First come the betrayal, the unkept promises, the lies. The more intense the relationship, the stronger the rejection and the broken heart. Then came the processing, the learning of lessons from each experience, along with the excruciating suffering of the feeling of abandonment, the devastation, obsession and grief. And the overwhelming loneliness.

Being a Bridge of Light, I could not comprehend the defeat of the relationship and the only way to overcome it was always going deep inside to acknowledge my own shadow, face it, talk to it and own it profoundly so I could re-associate all of those disowned parts of myself and discover again and again that the only true betrayal that existed was the one I had done to myself. I had given away my power to be loved, accepted, understood, respected, seen and heard as I am, instead of loving myself divinely.

Here is where the Frequencies of Golden Light speak to me.

It is in this domain that you are dearly loved. Do not diminish yourself. You've had a terrible, difficult year and you miss Mom. You are still grieving and you are taking your pain and grief out on what is happening in front of you and that has nothing to do with it.

The resting point of your true nature is where you want to be, in meditation it is your soul development that matters, in life, it is responding from your soul that matters. Nothing is outside of your own domain of being a wholehearted, wise, multidimensional being.

You are shedding an old identity that is now in a full-blown crisis, the manifestation of rage, irritability, neurosis, impatience, impulsiveness is coming out full-blown so you can see it and let it go. As a huge wind blowing through the breath of the divine cleanses the environment of toxic influences and shadows that lurk in the dark and have no power at all.

The original wound is completely exposed... the abandonment... the separation from the One.

There is a knowing, a longing, a fall into oblivious pain and suffering when as a fallen angel you just long for the supreme light where you belong.

Fallen from grace and Lucifer comparing himself to God, there are two and there is darkness. The shadow conquers and envelops the scenery like a veil of smoke. There is desolation and exhaustion of a long battle fought and lost. It is the final battle, an epic one between light and dark.

The battlefield is full of dead people, only more desolation. The remembrance of paradise absolutely lost. It is huge. It is the ashes, the total destruction; what helped you live and fight for your rights is completely obsolete now. You need to find compassion beneath the ashes. It lies covered beneath layers and layers of pain and suffering. The wars of ages repeating themselves in an apocalyptic view of sorts.

Devastation is absolute, you lost and you can let everything go now.

A little acorn seed is been planted and has the potential of a huge tree. The tree of life revealed and repeated as cycles of renewal again and again.

Just take care of that small seed now, nothing else.

Blessed be!

I realize that I am an independent soul that has no place in the family story of nightmares, money, possessions and control that rises from the illusion of that control. I burned to ashes and from them I rise as a new person. I choose to relate anew only through kindness and cut off all chords of ancient family history. It is done, now!

Stars are intelligent beings! The Frequencies of Golden Light are alive and vibrant, we bridge with your light. Indeed!

Technology is just an aid, it is not meant to substitute the sacredness of the soft technology you are as a human being. This is sacred, our humanness, indeed again!

You were greeting the old, the past, the wounds, the family, the difficulties, the conflicts the hurts. There is a baggage of experience now that you can cherish and with wondrous an curious eyes of a child you can go into the next phase of your life with a grateful heart as a wise, wholehearted multidimensional being and explore the many Bridges of Golden Light still to be opened and lived through as the Cosmos having a human experience in this lifetime being of service to the divine and when the time comes be ready to slip into the next transformation towards the light.

I will go on, allow and relax, listen, follow and repeat forever!

It is good to be alone
It is a model lifestyle
I walked this earth alone
I found the divine each turn

Coaching me where to go
I have never been alone
And never will be
I am a bridge of light with the divine in me
Cosmos having a human experience
Forever exploring infinity
Details are been taken care of
I am alive, electrical, transformative
I am a wholehearted, wise, multidimensional
being
I Am that I AM
And I love me divinely!
And I partnership with my divinity
To bring me to the safe harbors of life
I live with the wisdom of the ages
In each present moment
I am aware of the mystery of life
This is a privilege not many know
I acknowledge I am blessed!
And so it is!

Dear Beloved Bridges of Golden Light... what is the state of the union with the divine?

You need to be patient... the world is in havoc as a result of a profound transformation occurring at various levels of society that exploded with pandemic and is now pushing ahead. This is both at the collective level and at a personal level. There is correlation, as we are all interconnected. The only way we-you can manage is by being connected with that still, peaceful place inside, relaxing and being satisfied with being relaxed. All is well there/here you need to learn to be satisfied with being relaxed... just being relaxed. Why? Because all is well. You are moving forward, there has been a very difficult process of karmic disentanglement and now you can be content with that you can have the good life indeed! You have all the support you need and Mom as the Universal Mother is watching over you... Enjoy!

The Energy Work

———

The Energy Extension Incorporation (EEI) organization covers a live presence in more than 70 countries all over the world.

All EMF Balancing Technique® Practitioners have been certified by EEI and have completed the appropriate EMF Balancing Technique® training. EEI provides detailed training manuals and all the necessary tools to perform the EMF sessions as defined by the protocols of EEI and the technique's creator, Peggy Phoenix Dubro.

When giving an EMF Balancing Technique® session, you are a laser beam for the other person to enhance his or her empowerment and become more of who they are. You are working with the Universal Calibration Lattice® (UCL), a system in your energy anatomy, a hyperspatial, interdimensional construct: the toroid of consciousness, as Peggy now calls it.

When you give someone a session of the EMF Balancing Technique® you stand in your truth as a wise, wholehearted, multidimensional being to be more of who you are. The golden energy is the energy of wholeness and it permeates every cell of your body, every layer of DNA, every fiber of light of your being. It is a dome like no space and no time, where you expand into your multidimensionality. You go through a calibration process that includes the body prep, the clearing, the balancing, the closing... and the outcome is determined by your inner wisdom, your innate intelligence that regulates, balances, calibrates your energy exactly where and how you need it in this moment in time for your evolutionary process.

As the practitioner giving the session, you radiate your core energy, which calls the core energy of the person having the session with the intention of calibration. You are working with the fibers of light and energy of the UCL through very elegant Tai Chi movements on or over the body of the person on the massage table; they can feel their own energy as changes of temperature in the body, tingling, tickling and all of it as the result of human-to-human contact. My electromagnetic field activates yours and you accommodate your energy according to your inner wisdom.

This is why this technique is for everybody who wants to go deeper into the calibration and balancing of their own energy for their very personal intentions that are included in the wider intention of each session.

The Way of the Evolutionary is a way to consciously direct your energy to create the life of your choice. It is the whole journey you embark on if you decide to take the 12 sessions of the EMF Balancing Technique®.

The UCL we work with is a very complex structure made of light and energy and the very specific coordinates that Peggy offered, and it allows you to work in a very detailed way in the invisible realm with fibers, infinity loops and templates in layers and layers that connect the physical body and the emotional body even if you are working with the spiritual body. The electromagnetic system of the body is an extension of the nervous sympathetic and parasympathetic systems.

So yes, you are accessing very specific coordinates in the invisible realm that are part of the UCL. This is a system in your energy anatomy, parallel to the nadis in yoga or to the acupuncture strings, which is as complex as your biological system with organs, muscles, tissues, bones and various systems such as the circulatory one.

I offer the session in 3 modules of 4 sessions each:

1. Evolutionary Foundations: Phases I-IV

In Phases I-IV, you learn about the Universal Calibration Lattice®. In Phase I, your energy calibrates to balance your wisdom and your emotions. In Phase II, your energy calibrates to integrate the wisdom of your history. In Phase III, you focus on your Core Energy and being present in the now. In Phase IV, you give conscious intent as you calibrate your potential.

The first four sessions are the foundation of the

energy work and the intent of Phase I is to balance head and heart, a principle of all of this work. Phase II works with the long fibers in the back of the UCL, the past without limits of space or time for Self-Direction and Self-Support. Phase III in the Present works with the fibers of the sides of giving and receiving and with the Core energy in the present, the Now, the Spiritual Intelligence. Phase IV works with the fibers in the front of the UCL that are the Potential, the future.

2. Master in Practice: Phases V-VIII

In Phases V-VIII, you make conscious choices to practice the noble attributes of mastery in your daily life. Those choices create new energy patterns that continue to support you in your evolution.

3. Freedom! In The Energy of Love: Phases IX-XII

In Phases IX-XII, you further develop your ability to use the Third Lattice to manifest the energy of freedom within your being and your life.

The Third Lattice is the sum of your Universal Calibration Lattice® and the Calibration Lattice of every person, group, object and even abstract concept, like for example time. Does Lattice upon Lattice sound complicated? You can think of it as a unified, universal file system. Working with the Third Lattice helps you follow your evolutionary progress and increases your ability to make wise, conscious decisions in harmony with your intents and wishes.

The dynamics of fission and fusion are used repeatedly to create a unique and powerful energy of evolution.

The New Human is living within the energetic transformation of the New Earth! With this profound new expression of self, you will know you have transformed, and you will be equipped with new tools to manage your evolution.

As it is a technique, there are specific and precise steps and movements you perform in an organized fashion for each session. There are also specific phrases that the person can repeat after you, guiding their own energy. This increases the participation and focus of the session for the person.

When I started, training took a little longer because there were not as many tools to learn the technique as there are now. Now there are sophisticated, high-quality manuals, videos, teacher guides and audio materials. You can even learn the technique online: after teaching in more than 70 countries, Peggy has opened this possibility and there is a huge group of practitioners, teachers and teachers of teachers all over the world using this technique. There are translations of all these materials available in multiple languages along with new workshops, tools and activations that Peggy continues to offer those interested in living energetically aware.

I went all the way as I became a teacher of teachers for the technique. Besides translating for Peggy on stage live for many years in Spanish-speaking countries, I translated and refined the practitioner and teacher manuals countless times, as well as translating the audio, video and online materials and establishing a beautiful service for this technique taught all over the world in multiple languages.

As my personal process and spiritual path became my lifestyle and my way of relating to myself, others and the world, energy work has been my lighthouse for evolutionary development and my way of being of service. I have given thousands of sessions, formed many practitioners and taught profusely, even at a university (the Ibero-American University in Mexico), which exemplifies the high standard of our materials.

So it became my life, my work, my passion, my service, my travel around the world and my evolutionary process, which has brought me here. I have been doing this for more than 20 years now and evolved with it. It started out as a technique, and as a passionate student the calibration became deeper and stronger for me. You could follow the manual and the movements as taught and the exactitude was to hold the purity of the technique, no matter who gave it or where you took your session.

At the beginning it was a difficult call. Given my previous experience of emotional release method, shamanic practices and more free exploration in the energy world, I had to make a choice: the structured technique, with time, gave me inner freedom precisely because I could trust the process that was always bigger than us, the client, the student and me and expand in our multidimensionality in ways that I would never have imagined.

With time, devotion, dedication and a lot of practice and work in all areas of the EMF Balancing Technique® universe and working closely with Peggy not only as a student but as a translator, I became very proficient in the technique itself and built my own network of clients and students in Mexico City. I developed my own mastery as I developed the shift in perception that is the sensitivity that allows you to hear what is needed in the moment. You are the energy work itself, and the energy work is the master teacher.

This brought me to develop my own Bridges of Light method when I started to bridge the energy work with other spiritual paths. What I am sharing in this chapter is the original foundational energy work of the EMF Balancing Technique®, which constitutes the First Bridge of Golden Light that we do with our inner wisdom.

Validation

Besides doing the sessions, taking the trainings, reading additional books, conducting study and research to deepen my understanding, complementing it with hundreds of workshops and resources that resonated with me, my inquiries and what I was doing, there were always synchronicities that I needed to be open to and, of course, the pillars of light I discovered in my journeys.

One of those pillars at a scientific level, always

making a bridge with spirituality and the energy work, is Dr. Bruce Lipton. He is an internationally recognized leader in bridging science and spirit, a stem cell biologist and author of *The Biology of Belief,* who received Goi Peace Award in 2009. He says we are energy beings and we are visualized only because of the light reflected off the surface of our biology, that everything is energy and that energy signals are 100 times more efficient than chemical ones for controlling biological activity… meaning energy controls who and what we are.

Additionally, as Einstein said: "The field is the sole governing agency of the particle." Life is controlled by energy, invisible fields that surround us. Matter is just one form of energy. Energy shapes matter (biology), quantum physics controls our life and the mind creates our life experiences. Change your mind and you change the characteristics of your life. Mind = consciousness.

I always find in these pioneers inspiration and validation for passionately doing my work, and I strongly suggest to always nurture whatever passion you have with complementary resources. Indeed!

I also found inspiration in shamanism. In his teachings and writings, Alberto Villoldo, founder of the world-renowned Four Winds Society and of the Light Body School, shares the experience of infinity and its ability to heal and transform us, to free us from the temporal chains that keep us fettered by illness, old age and disease. He defines shamans as living in a world where the creator is not separate from the creation, Heaven is not separate from Earth and spirit and matter infuse each other. There is no division between the body and the spirit, nor between the visible world of form and the invisible world of energy. I confirm this with this poem of mine.

The Lady of the Lake

Emptiness has a face
Grace manifesting the divine
The slow deep breaths
Open the warmth in the body
The light is on
The image starts to form
Water becomes still
Becomes mirror-like
The reflection gets clearer
The face shines through the lake
It has my face!
In the space of No-thing
I recognize a tear
The lake flows through me
In the stillness I cry.

Magic happens and it is very real. We are not fixing anyone as there is nothing to be fixed. As a practitioner, I facilitate the empowerment of the person that calibrates their own energy in response to the human-to-human connection that functions as a laser beam for inner wisdom to guide the energy to where the person needs it, determining the results and outcomes of the session. So the person is saying yes to him or herself in each session, to become more of who they are.

This, of course, brings sometimes miraculous transformations and healings, but we do not announce the technique as such, as the results are very personal, and the aim is always to facilitate for the person the balance of their personal energy. When you give an EMF session, you facilitate the empowerment of a person working human-to-human with the UCL®. This causes changes of temperature in the body, tingling, tickling… these been the signs that the energy of the person, his or her inner wisdom is directing the energy where the person needs it.

We are all unique and interconnected, so working with the UCL (like meditating with the asanas in yoga) you step into a place where no time or space exists… that dome of light where we speak the language of energy. All our bodies—the physical, the emotional, the energetic—are interconnected; we work with the energy body and all bodies are affected. We jump in, dive in and we are in the Cosmic Lattice where each one expands and calibrates their own Universal Calibration Lattice® in their own way. Like a laser light, you as the practitioner act as the reminder of the wholeness that we are when we work through the different layers of the UCL, always in accordance with the inner wisdom of the person involved.

Lately, Peggy has been giving Activations to the world online and she says that the UCL is evolving as we traverse these transformative and auspicious times.

We are all interconnected; the resonance and the frequency of all the body of work of the EMF expands and when you give the first 12 sessions the energy is even stronger, more expansive and coherent. It really makes sense that the UCL is evolving too, as it is part of this great evolution momentum that the world—and all of humanity—is going through right now.

An Example of EMF Work

I finished with my client the last session of what I call the First Bridge of Light module, which consists of the 12 original traditional sessions of the EMF Balancing Technique®. Due to the Covid lockdown, we did the whole 12 sessions online: one hour or more, once a week. The 12th session was special: you rarely encounter such a special individual. You are always a teacher but also a student of the energy work when you give the sessions: you are calibrating yourself at the same time. It is very safe work, as we do not mix the energies of the practitioner and the client; there are specific movements to uphold healthy boundaries so that the energies are not compromised. There are movements you use to disconnect in respect during the session, whether it is in person or virtual. There is no space, no time distance when working with energy. We are all in the present eternal moment where all the miracles happen and we access our multidimensionality.

So this special one was very familiar with the outer space experiences with other beings of light (and not-so-bright ones) and has battled all his life to survive in this dense 3D world we live in. He is a successful entrepreneur with a very rich spiritual life. The work we did gave him more clarity and helped him sort out his own energies entangled with old defensive habits—he was hurt early in life: diagnosed with autism at birth and unable to speak in his early years, he was mistreated and bullied. Somehow, because of his connection with his expanded consciousness, he was able to find his functionality in this lifetime and the work we did helped him remember who he really is, finding peace in himself. He learned to open his heart again: he became softer and discovered another dimension of his body that was unknown for him. No wonder one of the main statements of the EMF work is that "the key to freedom is to be fully present in your body:" your body is multidimensional and we are just learning to use it as such.

Peggy has always said that we are all channels learning to channel more of who we are in the body, through the body. The universe could not otherwise flow through us. We do that with the magic of our bodies… we are the magic! We are extraordinary human beings precisely because we are in a body.

He was harmonizing himself with the calibrations, channeling himself and expressing the enormous wisdom of the ages from all these lifetimes and adventures of cosmic resonance. I have always said that "Family" is meeting… I mean your cosmic Family, and yes, this is validation once more that we have a mission as Bridges of Light in bringing the divine to the daily lives of a conflicted and troubled humanity, to find our way back home to the peace and unity that many of us long for.

So it has been a wonderful journey through these 12 phases of remembrance in the energy of love and, at the same time, it is only the beginning of more cycles of transformation for oneself and others. Time to rest and enjoy the Calibration—Celebration! Once again! Infinite Gratitude!

We are Bridges of Light between higher energies and the energies of the earth. The flow of energy in our core is the way the universe flows through us and the infinity loops is the way we bridge our energies and communicate back and forth with the rest of the universe horizontally with co-creators, dancing, drawing more Bridges of Light... as we are all shades of light expressing uniquely.

We form a wonderful tapestry of the Cosmos when each of us in our human form expresses the unique piece of the puzzle we are... we enhance the divine presence on earth and our humanity enlarges the divine Cosmos with waves of light all over.

Bridges upon bridges of highways of light into all corners and dimensions of the Cosmos that vibrate in different sounds and frequencies of unworldly and infinite shades of light that you can find throughout the universes. Our personal UCL as our mothership to go to each of these dimensions that we explore as the multidimensional beings we are.

This happens in each and every session, where the underlying peace filled empowerment is present and the harmony of the ages helps us heal our small, troubled human minds. We acknowledge our multidimensionality and learn to be grateful as the universe is speaking to us all the time even in the more miniscule aspects of reality unfolding in our earthly existence. We heal ourselves locally and universally and discover each time new horizons where the lessons learned make a future from our healed past in the expression of wholeness in the present moment.

In this dome of light we stand in when in session, no time or space. Only the profound and sacred intimate feeling of our infinite selves touching each other. The power of love shows that it's mighty: the feeling is strong, pure and we become the pure channels and conduits of the light of the divine to empower our humanness with the energy of love. We enlighten love frequencies that shine brighter when we calibrate them sensing a response in every cell of the body that slowly start to vibrate higher. Sometimes the physical body takes a while to adjust so we take care of it with rest, drinking water, baths and, if possible, we write, journal to register the changes, the quantum leaps, the transformations, the evolutionary leaps that occur so when we meet again we reflect with profound core wisdom what has transpired in the sacred journey of calibrating ourselves.

We find meaning and truth with compassion of our human weaknesses and faults and we are enlightened by the pure light of divine love. We thrive in enhancing ourselves as pure conduits of that light forgetting about the analytical mind and the stubbornness of ego that wants to interfere and retake control.

Gently, sometimes more forcefully, we name the transformations of self and this makes it easier to recognize the adjustments we can make in our daily lives, as we are more aware of our energies and how they work so we can live more energetically aware. We learn to speak the language of energy and include in our ordinary moments the magic of our multidimensionality and we remember we are those magnificent and brilliant bridges of the light of the divine in this earthly existence. We grow and we smile more.

We live in this magical universe where Peggy shared with her experience in Paris with a huge group of people, about the EMF work and how under certain circumstances subatomic particles are able to communicate instantly with one another, no matter how far apart; how separateness is an illusion on a deeper level of reality as particles are not individual, separate entities. The universe is a gigantic, splendid, detailed hologram. We are part of a hologram.

She continues: As human beings there is a neurosynchronization with the environmental rhythm around us. Night and day. This neurosynchronization with our surroundings helps shape our perception of one reality, to go into new levels of coherence. Creative chaos to co-creative coherence to accomplish in the world in this great evolution.

Lynne McTaggart confirms that the real language of the human body is frequency. All living things are communicating via light, within and between—the Bridge of Light metaphor is not exclusive to me. She continues and speaks of tiny currents of light coming out of our DNA and how the biophotons are ordered light, the most coherent light in nature. Light waving at the same light in the same amplitude, together acting as a giant wave as the signal gets stronger. We are sending and receiving, we communicate with our environment in a Morse code of light emissions. We are light beings communicating with our environment every moment. We are energy systems.

After all, spectroscopy is the study of light through light-matter interactions and we, as conduits of the beyond in our multidimensional capacity of dimensions beyond the ordinary, filter them through as real possibilities for this world.

We have a beautiful communication posture that we use in the EMF work that is simple and collects in a succinct and clear way all that has been shared. It is a practice we can cultivate to have clearer and whole-hearted communications with each other.

This you learn when you do the training to become a practitioner of the EMF work and it is a very practical tool that puts in practice all the theoretical principles of quantum physics. Peggy calls herself a practical mystic, and the EMF Balancing Technique® is a practical tool for the expansion of consciousness in our daily lives… Indeed!

For Phases V through VIII of the EMF Balancing Technique® that Peggy channeled and delivered in her trainings as we went along, I must recognize that I had put myself in a privileged position for the different aspects of the work I did for the organization over more than 20 years. One of many events I participated in was the training Peggy gave in Buenos Aires, Argentina. There were more than 80 people from more than 9 countries (Chile, Colombia, Venezuela, Uruguay and Mexico, but also Denmark, Australia and the United States) taking the Practicing Mastery course. That's what Peggy called these four phases: "Practice Mastery." The small staff was very busy and excited receiving the practitioners and teachers of the previous phases that Peggy had already trained around the world, handing out materials and working a lot as always taking care of everything.

For me it was always a privilege and an honor to translate Peggy on stage. I learned a lot. Being in Peggy's energy is very stimulating and a lot of fun. From the theory to the practical work and the question and answers, there is never a dull moment and time flies. The only permanent thing is Peggy's smile and loving action. We all walked the talk, as they say. She is a role model for practicing mastery and inspires every one of us along the way. At the end of the day, we were all proud to answer whenever someone asked us if we were still into that "weird" stuff we used to do: "oh, yes, we work with the Universal Calibration Lattice®, an interdimensional hyperconductor in time and space coordinates, here and now…"

Even more people came to another workshop she gave. We were about 130: our colleagues had organized programs and articles about the importance of Peggy's presence in Córdoba, Argentina interest and attendance soared following media, university TV and magazine interviews with Peggy and her husband

Stephen Dubro (the other half of the work) as he took care of general questions and cheers from EMF practitioners and teachers. It is always a joy to explore our multidimensionality as holographic humans, deepening our understanding of who we really are. This was 2005, if I am not mistaken. And this is only one of my many travels and personal experiences with EEI, which filled my life with joy and wonder. I have always been amazed by the power of the energy of love that drives this work.

Phases V-VIII: Practice of Mastery

These 4 phases have a slightly different structure than the first 4. They are the next step after having trained and practiced Phases I-IV, which were the foundations of the energy work.

There are beautiful illustrated cards with a simple explanation to stimulate the intuitive and logical sense of the person that is choosing the cards representing the attributes of mastery. These are only 44 (though of course there are many more) of the noble attributes of being a human being such as compassion, courage, patience, harmony and unconditional love, which you select, giving them a certain order: that will be the way the practitioner activates these attributes during the session, after answering deep questions channeling through specific energies. You respond to the resonance according through your inner wisdom, for the resonance is within all of us. We entrain and we raise our frequency and we co-create together throughout

Phases V-VIII, synchronizing with the energy of masters in practice.

This brings out more of the original resonance of the being and then continues to be practiced in everyday life. An important step for refining the qualities or attributes of being a Bridge of Light is the training of Phases V-VIII, called Practice of Mastery, in which we activate the noble attributes of mastery in the energetic body.

As always, in the EMF work you first work with yourself so you can then offer it to others. Therefore, here I use poems to share my transformation while taking the sessions of my experience with the attributes activated in my energy body in each phase. It was 2003 when I took this training in Sedona, Arizona, with Peggy and I will never forget the major stepping stone it was for my work and my own development.

These poems came out as prayers that for a long time I continued to repeat for embodying these attributes of mastery, which, of course, were reinforced each time I gave and still give a session. As in the EMF Balancing Technique® you calibrate yourself as you are giving the energy session as there is no compromising the energies as there are beautiful "disconnect" movements in respect that allow for that.

Poems/Prayers for Phases V-VIII

Phase V

Infinite Self with Infinite Love, please give me:

Courage to trust the process unconditionally
Openness to the unknown
Sincerity in accepting actual limitations
Honesty to recognize where I stand
Permanent initiation even in the small
Transformation with integration
Flexibility for smoothing corners
Forgiveness, looking at the star within others and me
Humor to have a good laugh at myself
Creativity in expanding horizons
Freedom to fly within

Phase VI

Infinite Self with Infinite Compassion, please give me:
Patience for celebrating delays
Neutrality for detaching, recognizing the appropriateness of what happens in my life with a cosmic perspective,
In balance—equilibrium with compassion, accepting the universal concert
Finding the right tune to enhance its beauty
With humility in recognizing the drop of the ocean I AM
Communicating my uniqueness with respect to others
Without judgment and grateful for the learning in every interaction
Expressing the joyfulness of it all
In a friendly and considerate manner

With readiness for more generosity!

Phase VII

Infinite Self with Infinite Presence, help me:
Deepen my personal expression
From the stillness of my being
With the purity of my soul
Focusing to see clearly what to do next in my co-creative process
With the security of feeling safe
Trusting my own guidance
Generating all kinds of abundance I need
Accessing my own inner sight
To have the necessary insight and wisdom
Using my intuition to achieve the understanding
To be able to discern my heart path and solve my challenges
With mindfulness and self-acceptance
Recognizing my worth and abilities to act in
each circumstance in my life
For the greater good of all involved

Phase VIII

Infinite Self with Infinite Wisdom, inspire me:
To offer to the world the integration of my wholeness
With unconditional love and the persistence of the ages
In the harmony needed for living an enlightened life

Based on insight, intuition and discernment
With the power to act with integrity and
knowledge
Offering my skills with commitment to my heart
desires
Trusting the light
For the peacefulness in our world

After the training, having worked and bridged this journey with my Infinite Self, I wrote this poem:

My Journey Home in a Fast Track

Suddenly I was in the hall of honor
Caressed by the angels
Infinite rainbow core light
With spiraling colored spheres all around me
I could feel the freshness of the spring water and
the cascade
The dome of light with all the other infinites
around me
The golden and platinum fibers and circuits
overflowing the horizon
The greenness of nature
All my seen and unseen friends
The crystalline structure of prisms and templates
sparkling everywhere
Pure bliss!
Pure light!
Pure love!
I remember, I AM
Suddenly I was home

And have always been
And will always be
And so it is!

Phases IX-XII

The inner universe where I live is just a speck in the huge journey of the soul. *You are the Universe!* In that Universe the sun warms me up. The glowing, shimmering, vibrant and brilliant reflections of light bring you the remembrance of other journeys of the soul within other universes.

When we work with the Universal Calibration Lattice®, our toroid of consciousness, and we acknowledge our relationships with others we work with another layer of consciousness where my UCL and your UCL form one huge UCL. It is the Lattice of Relationships, where we can continue moving our own electrical charges and we alter or modify the Third Lattice.

You can only change the charges of your own lattice, but that will affect the Lattice of the relationship. We can be very specific when we work with this lattice as we can chose one relationship we want to focus on. Lattices upon lattices are all interconnected: working with one, we affect them all.

In our universe, we can sort things out and use it as a universal filing system where we have organized experiences with so much knowledge and wisdom that helps us do the job of re-inventing ourselves into the next phases of life.

In Phase IX, we work with the template of the

Universal Human as a portal into our relationship lattice. In Phase X, we continue with the templates of infinite archetypes of masculine and feminine energies that we as humans all have: the Universal Parents. In Phase XI, we work with another archetype, the Universal Beloved; lastly, Phase XII deals with the Emergent Evolutionary, which continues the expansion of consciousness into the beyond.

These calibrations allow us to journey deep into the universe of our relationships worlds integrating them into the next steps of our evolutionary process. Magic happens again, as in every energy session, in the energy of Infinite Love that expands life on earth as the presence of our soul comes through more transparently in our daily lives.

Calibration—Celebration! That is my motto in the EMF Balancing Technique® work and it holds true for each session, each workshop, each training.

I went all the way, becoming a teacher of teachers, translating, working directly with Peggy and her staff, and we continue to be very close.

Now, she has gone online and continues to evolve and offer master activations and trainings to strengthen our Universal Calibration Lattice®, our toroid of consciousness, so we learn to live energetically aware... and the original, traditional 12 phases of the EMF Balancing Technique® are the foundation of it all. It is also the foundation of all my Bridges of Light body of work, which I'll delve into in the next chapter.

There are many sessions, workshops, activations and trainings offered in this work that keeps deepening and evolving. You can explore them all in Peggy's website (see the list of links and literature at the end of the book!)—at the bottom of the homepage you can find a book the EMF teachers gifted Peggy for her 70th birthday gathering dozens of testimonies to honor her work and legacy, titled *How I changed my life with the EMF Balancing Technique.*

So I did this work of the EMF Balancing Technique® for more than 20 years and I continue to do it now: it became the first Module of the Body of work of Bridges of Light, where, as I said before, you build the Bridge of Light with your inner wisdom after going through the 12 sessions of the EMF Balancing Technique®.

You can do all 12 sessions or decide to take only the first four and it will be very gratifying for your learning to live energetically aware and have more clarity in your evolutionary process about the life you want to create.

You can choose to repeat whichever of the 12 sessions whenever you want, as they become personal tools for your own evolution or expansion of consciousness.

You will find that you can continue the work with me in the next modules of Bridges of Light, which I will explain in the next chapter; alternatively, you can decide you want to learn to give the sessions and take the trainings or explore other workshops. You will always find these foundations of this energy work in all of them, as it is the doorway to a more expanded consciousness indeed!

CHAPTER SIX:

The Body of Work

——

The Enlightened One

Sparkles of light tickle my Spirit
They land in the playground of Infinite
Possibilities
The heart beats faster and louder…
I hear songs of jubilation…
I am new
The Universe flows through me
I choose which one of my freedoms I engage
today
I meet with my Expanded Self in the Field
And we play…
Crystalline communication, transparent au-
thenticity and tender compassion are needed to
interact with the Gods in disguise we all are.
I open the doors and the light comes in…
Coloring with brilliance next stages of
illumination
I turn on my inner switch
And there is Light!

Now I can create the most enlightened life!
In a dome of no time and no space
I access my multidimensionality
All is wrapped in shimmering light
I forever forget to turn off the switch!
Infinite Gratitude!
I jump into the field of consciousness and I meet you there
where expansion abides
We float in the cosmic rivers with ease and grace
Reinventing our lives
In the energy of love and excitement
In our awakened world.

My destiny is to build Bridges of Light. This is what I realized after working for more than 20 years with the EMF Balancing Technique® and all of the tools that continued to evolve from it.

After working with so many clients and students and presenting the energy work to so many people and seeing the results in the expansion of consciousness for each individual no matter where they came from, their age, their gender, their religious affiliation, their habits or addictions or whatever else, I continued to evolve with this work myself... from the very beginning. That's what I love about this work: I facilitate calibration for others while at the same time calibrating myself.

As multidimensional beings, as the unique expression of the universe, each person will calibrate according to their inner wisdom, so the results are guaranteed. They will become clearer in their evolutionary process. In this way, I myself also continue to evolve. There were many who, after doing the 12 phases of the EMF plus session 13 and repeating many of the sessions to deepen the experience, wanted to go even further with the energy work. That's what I did: I kept studying and deepening my own practice and discovery of paths leading me to develop my spiritual life, my passion for the divine and my life of service that go hand in hand as each one nurtures the other.

Peggy evolved too, going online and offering more tools born of the foundational work of the EMF. I stayed in contact with all this while at the same time being involved with the work and practices of Conscious Evolution that Barbara Marx Hubbard was sharing online. I had the privilege of meeting her in person when she came to a summit in Monterrey (in Mexico): our intense sharing was a delight I'll never forget. She was extraordinarily brilliant, alive, inspiring and we had a bridge of resonance that I treasure to this day. I deeply studied all her books and facilitated workshops with her and her sister Patricia Ellsberg, from *Emergence—The Shift from Ego to Essence*.

I was passionately involved in that work. It resonated and complemented my energy work and benefited my spiritual growth. I was merging the experiences I had with the energy work with a Bridge of Light between them. It was a feedback loop that made me grow immensely both emotionally and spiritually and I wanted to share it and offer it as a follow-up to my clients.

Hence, after the first module of 12 EMF sessions developing the Bridge of Light with the inner wisdom, the second module came to be: a Bridge of Light with Essence, also through 12 sessions that started with the I Phoenix energy work of a new tool Peggy offered and the bridging with Barbara's *Emergence—The Shift From Ego to Essence*. In this second module I was bridging the work with Conscious Evolution. For these 12 sessions, I worked with clients one-on-one or in small groups, and it turned out to be magical—as always.

Journaling, a major tool of self-empowerment, has always been the way to be connected with Spirit, Soul, the Divine; this connection is the basis of my work with myself and others.

The strengthening with the connection with the Divine as Bridges of Light was growing and in this way the third module of the Body of Work of the Bridges of Light developed with an offering now of another 12 sessions where the energy work of the Waves of Peggy was bridged with 52 codes for *Conscious Self Evolution—A Process of Metamorphosis to Realize our Full Potential Self*. Barbara's book that I translated into Spanish and worked beautifully for the Bridge of Light with the Universal Self now expanding our soul's work with the spiritual journaling of course as an important tool to register, follow up and expand the deepening of our connection with the divine. People loved it.

Automatic Writing/Spiritual Journaling

Learn to love both the form and the formless! Life

meeting life. From the transparent awareness of abiding in the light you slowly come back into a denser, more fully formed physical anchored life in the body and on the planet.

The density goes deep into the core of the Earth and there is light there too. It is warmer and fiery and here we touch the dark light of the womb of the Infinite Self that meets the womb of planet Earth and makes it our home for now.

We have lived many lives down here. Again and again, we come and go. Lifetime after lifetime, we witness the evolution of nature and life meeting life when we melt into the mist of a denser, more obscure environment; other worlds are evolving in the underground caves and you can sense the beating of the hearts.

We are all one and it is a collective call, like a drum calling us all to take care of our home in space. The inside of these worlds is your outside—but it is not so different from the inside of your inner world. All these different spaces and shades of light are what make a beautiful tapestry of life meeting life in wonder and awe.

The newness and the discovery keep going every moment in a continuum that never stops. Creation is a constant evolution and reshaping of different forms of life that meet. The vibrational frequencies of light on this dimension are as translucid messages from beyond.

There are different ways and paths for the creative illumination process of bringing the new to form in this dimension. Generally it has to do with the different vibrations of the energy of love.

You start to listen to the subtle sounds and whispers of the soul that reflect in the body and by grace, imagination and feeling start to bring out a manifestation in form of music, painting, sculpture, poems. Words are special as there is a whole bubbling process between the world and the dimensions going on.

The hand writes and it is not you writing... it comes from a vast ocean of stillness and awareness that on the way to the page with a speed of light delineates bridges between dimensions that then show up written on a blank page. It is a weird path of wiring where the light seems to conduct itself as waves coming through and appearing as words.

There is an exhilarating sensation as it feels that it comes from the unknown and the meaning and sense are a message from other dimensions.

It is life meeting life in multidimensionality; we are going back and forth, crossing dimensions and illuminating the constant creation of worlds.

Energy Psychology

As some clients wished to continue growing and advancing their evolutionary process with me, I worked with them in the second and third modules. Here is part of a testimony written by one client, Casilda, which continued to inspire me to share more modules as the next building blocks for more Bridges of Light.

Since I began the experience of the EMF Balancing Technique® and, later on, with the tools that Adriana provided, I can honestly say that my life and my Being entered a new halo of clarity: the clarity of knowing that each person is able to co-create their own life as he/she wishes. This work implies trusting, but also taking action. I act, both wishing and building my wishes. Nowadays, I do not know another way to be responsible for myself. I started in one place on my map and consciously shifted to another, more loving, luminous and integral. In this sense, I can say that the work with Adriana, which she calls Bridges of Light, changed my life… and I am hugely grateful for this.

She also said she had other alternatives she could work with, and the reason she chose to work with me—and she has a been a very dedicated student—is that she saw that everything I taught was from experience. I had lived it, gone through the process, learned the lessons and only then shared them.

That was the final test for her, to commit to such deep work for so many years. We are good friends now, and I am proud to have been part of her life. She found the love of her life, married and has 2 lovely kids. She never stopped dancing: she is a pioneer teacher and dancer in new ways of flamenco and "movement of spirit." She went to live in another state away from Mexico City to find new possibilities of community and schooling for her children, and explores modern ways of parenting and living in a creative way.

I am so grateful to her for her commitment to her own life and for having allowed me to accompany her and see the beautiful Bridge of Light she has become. With tears in my eyes, I can say to you now that this is the only thing that makes sense to me in a life of service, of bringing and sharing the Divine, in this lifetime with other souls that are determined to blossom and create magic here on Earth.

This cannot be done in any other way than living it for myself first and sharing it for the greater good of all sentient beings. This is my inspiration for developing the body of work of Bridges of Golden Light.

At some point, I realized that as a coach of energy consciousness, as a practitioner and teacher of the EMF Balancing Technique® working with clients and teaching the technique to many students, continuing to guide those who wanted to keep exploring their path of spiritual growth with me, I was in a new field of practice that can be called energy psychology. That is how I frame my work with Bridges of Light modules.

Einstein said that the field or mind, is the sole governing agency of the particle, body. Life is controlled by energy, invisible fields that surround us. Matter is just a unique form of energy. Energy shapes matter (biology). Quantum physics controls our life. The mind creates our life experiences. Change your mind and you change the characteristics of your life. Mind equals consciousness here in these affirmation that gave me the validation always to continue bridging the energy work with other works that now included more sophisticated aspects of mind.

This is an extract of my dialogue with the

Frequencies of Golden light with which I communicate (taken from my journal):

The space is green and the light... is brilliant...

How do I enjoy bridging the light? What do you mean?

Well, reflections. My core energy reflects the wholeness of your core energy and we are one when sitting in awareness.

What you do is energy psychology, as you explore the experience with others and find the root of a shadow by the illumination of the deeper truth where the being rests like a clay sculpture that finds its way and slowly shows its final face. It is the process of creation.

With the co-creator, we discover a repeating pattern that bothers him or her, and focusing our attention we can illuminate the twisting swirls of the soul that, like a labyrinth, brings us back to a clear path of truth within oneself and allows for building the Bridges of Light with others, a clearer path to relate to each other. We explore together a wide, open field of awareness where we abide when focusing on energy work.

It is a world of wonder, of light and shadows, which lets calm, coherent feelings come through with pristine clarity of spirit, present and expanding each time with the multidimensional metaphor of Bridges of Light being built. Drawn in awareness, as paths to clarity of the life lived and the truthfulness and realness of experience.

Essentially, energy psychology is an approach to psychotherapy that involves coaching and healthcare treatment to work on the body-mind connection. This is helping a lot of people all over the world deal with trauma, stress and more.

Dr. Bruce Lipton discovered the importance of something like energy psychology when working in the field of epigenetics. Epigenetics argues that the choices we make in our lives influence our genes and our cells more than our DNA does. This field is gaining importance and more and more scientists are seeing that it is indeed the case. Energy psychology works with that principle, helping improve the lives of individuals, as well as their minds and bodies.

In his book *The Biology of Belief,* Lipton looks at epigenetics and how genes are controlled by signals that don't come from the cell but from outside of it. He didn't just come up with this on the fly: this idea is grounded in his decades of experience as a cell biologist, as well as with quantum physics and his deep understanding of the processing system of cells.

The cell membrane, which is the outer layer of the cell, actually looks a lot like a computer chip. It's the brain of the cell. While researching epigenetics at the Stanford University School of Medicine from 1987 to 1992, he found that the environment outside the membrane operated through the membrane and controlled the behavior of the cells, turning them on and off.

Energy psychology works with this concept. By influencing the outside environment, you can actually influence your own genetics. This means you can greatly improve your mind-body connection, your life and your happiness. It is becoming increasingly popular as people see its huge benefits: when your mind and body are in harmony, everything else just seems to fall into place. That is what energy psychology is all about, and what Casilda's testimony reveals about the Bridges of Light.

Bridges of Light: Modules 1, 2, 3 and 4

The structure of the body of work that became the Bridges of Light as such had already started with the 12 sessions of the EMF Balancing Technique®.

This is the first module of 12 sessions. The core thread in each of these sessions is the building of **Module 1 – Bridge of Light with Inner Wisdom**.

From here on, the next modules are also the building of another Bridge of Light through building blocks of 12 sessions each. These sessions are the practical tools that help you, the client, undergo your evolutionary process expanding your consciousness and deepening your understanding and clarity of the spiritual work of Bridges of Light. The life force within us is our connection to the infinite and that includes every potential for healing.

So you become the bridge, the clearest open vessel for divinity to express itself in this world through you, and you nourish yourself as a unique expression of the divine to be manifested in this lifetime.

The second module of 12 sessions is **Module 2**

– Bridge of Light with Essence. The tools for each session in this Module are the iPhoenix energy sessions by Peggy Phoenix Dubro (a modality of energy work) with the 10 chapters of *Emergence—The Shift from Ego to Essence*.

So with written materials of the journey from ego to essence that you review and journal about in each session, with the bridging of the energy work and specific meditations you journey from Ego to Essence building the next expanded Bridge of Light for your own life. This is a very personal and customized process guided by me, which reflects and empowers your Essence—you are always becoming more of who you are, I just facilitate this process.

I must say this is not a linear process. What I mean is that you do not necessary need to go through the Modules with the 12 sessions in a linear fashion. You could take the 4 first sessions of Module 1 and that is it. One session a week is great for the unraveling of the benefits for each session, and here also it is just a suggestion as each person will have their own needs of time and use of their resources and this is fine. Another person would like to come in for the first time in Module 2 and do those 4 or 8 or 12 sessions, as that is what they needed in that moment of their evolutionary process. The person (or persons, as these sessions can be done in small groups) have always an amplified conversation with me at the beginning of our encounter to determine what is best for them wherever they find themselves in their evolutionary process.

In the third module of 12 sessions, you continue

to expand your consciousness into **Module 3 – Bridge of Light with Universal Self.** Our tools here in these sessions are the energy modality of The Waves by Peggy Phoenix Dubro and we bridge that work with the *52 Codes for Conscious Self Evolution* book by Barbara Marx Hubbard, appropriately subtitled *A Process of Metamorphosis to Realize Our Full Potential Self.*

Here again we use your journaling as a main tool that at this level expands into spiritual journaling. This is the main thread that bridges the 12 sessions and allows you to connect with your Universal Self experientially.

Even if there is a very specific structure for the work for every session, that usually goes from one hour to one hour fifteen, it also is a very customized system dictated by the inner needs of the client of their own evolutionary process. In the work we do we never use the idea of fixing anything as this would imply there is something broken. We believe in the expansion of consciousness in the unique way that each person needs it and I am a facilitator for that process to unfold.

So from here on and from this conviction I continued to create more building blocks for this body of work. The fourth module is **Module 4 – Bridge of Light with the Whole Being**. Peggy was already sharing her master activation trainings online to strengthen the Universal Calibration Lattice®, our toroid of consciousness.

As Peggy always says, this system is an extension of consciousness elegantly designed to support us as we continue to evolve. She sees us all as channels learning to channel more of who we are. In this Master Activation, you activate the 8 Gates of Universal Ancestry within this Lattice.

This is the energy modality we use in Module 4 and we bridge it with Shadow Work, another fundamental tool in our path of enlightenment. Spiritual journaling continues to be a main tool for each of these 12 sessions to dive deep into your evolutionary path.

The Shadow Work of this module is framed within the tools provided by Andrew Harvey: it can go into more not only personal but collective shadows, depending on the person I am working with. The seven shadows available to explore in this case are: unworthiness, narcissism, fear of taking a stand, love of comfort, traumatization, woundology and the golden shadow. We work with the counterpart of each shadow—the process of going from endarkenment to engoldenment.

The deep diving into your own shadows is bridged with the energy work to strengthen our own light and resonance and elevate our frequencies towards higher dimensions of being: we need to go deep into Shadow Work. Here, journaling becomes even more important: registering your spiritual journey and the reflection of working together in the sessions, as we share our voyage into the shadows.

Just Falling... Just Arising...

I fall from the edge of the Earth
Into an ocean of expanded consciousness
where stillness and silence abide.
I stand in the horizon where sky and ocean meet
In the middle of crystalline waters
I hold the Sun in one hand and the Moon in the
other
Directing the symphony of Cosmos.
I am guided to the cliff of awareness
Falling into the energy of love that has a pinkish
hue
I float and feel cozy, cradled in the arms of the
dharma
I rest wrapped in grace and bliss.
Every morning I engage in a dance with you
I feel you feeling me feeling you
An infinity loop of giving and receiving
No beginning... no end...
Melting and knowing God through the breath
that bubbles in me
Just rising... just falling...
I am awake, I am electrical, I am alive!

Trust the Process

You can trust the process. We all go through our
own dark night of the soul—probably more than
once—and we come out the other side.

Human beings have a tendency to go to the dark
side. We talk to gods for confirmation, but it is really

just our own thirst for power that we are talking to: it is a human distortion. We do this instead of surrendering to the divine in each one of us, sacrificing the ego and its ambitious need for control and power, making space for something else to manifest through us.

I am already a beacon of light, I am awakened, I am a midwife for illumination. I've always been. I help light up the darkness so the sorting out can happen. Relaxing in silence and speaking from emptiness without effort, focusing, listening to what wants to come through.

I have gone through my own dark night of the soul, and I knew that working through your own shadows is an ongoing process.

I see a cave where I find the cracks... that is your shadow...

The five shadows: disbelief, denial, dread, disgust, death... the glory of enlightenment where you are shown the shadows and you are working through them at the same time.

The smoky, black sphere emerging and dissolving in the clear, blue sky of the heart bathed with the golden sunlight that is always shining.

The transition is through Dante's inferno and you can see that below the flames lies a frozen lake.

That is why we meet at the river with the warmth of the sun shining over you, and you can see us in the glimmering light over the waters that flow incessantly with a calm feeling of joy, an all-is-well sensation of life unfolding.

No cracks in the river. Come out of the cave to the green lawn, to the wooden bench under the huge tree where you can rest in the peace and glory of the magnificence and wonder of—and with—life.

As in the story of the resurrection of Christ, you cannot bypass the crucifixion, as the transfiguration comes from the transit from "they do not know what they are doing" to "take this cup away from me" and then to Mary and Mary Magdalene crying under the cross… and then discovering the resurrected body, the revelation that the Sun is always shining. The cave where the body and the shroud are found are part of the mystery: how does Christ get out of the body, of the cave, and become the luminous body that then appear to the apostles?

You are already the body of light, no longer bound by the body. It is the human form that looks like a limitation. Why do we see in the political arena the distortion of the truth, the misunderstandings of democracy, the slaughtering of reality, facts and truths? It is unbelievably disgusting, and that is when we lose faith in humanity. How can you love them? They do know what they are doing: the destruction of the good, the truth and the beautiful. It is horrendous! And so painful. They forget the sacredness of life and they do not know—or they forget—that the Sun is always shining.

When you work with your shadows you remind yourself how to maintain the intimacy, integrity and depth of interaction needed for the revelation of the magnificence of being and life, and expand it…you go through it all to come out the other side.

The paradox is that in resting in calm abiding presence, no pushing, you let go of your exasperation, irritability and frustration wanting to push through it all at once and you embrace your dark places and shadows. You discover who you are at the bottom of the ocean, in your depth, and emerge as the person on the surface, awake in a tired body.

The bigger Higher Self helps you to let the potentials come through into the world, consciousness attunes to the moment. Allow the highest possibility that wants to come through you to fulfill itself without resistance.

So working with our shadows and at the same time doing the energy work of strengthening our Universal Calibration Lattice®, our body of light, our toroid of consciousness, our electromagnetic field, you transcend it and come out the other side transfigured to help others bridge the light.

If you are a Bridge of Light it is because you have traversed the darkness and come out the other side. It is the black holes of the universe, holding the tension of extremes and bridging the light, the golden light that you pull in, that showers you and enlightens your divine nature to be expressed in the world as the love you are as the light of source you are. This is the Bridge of Light you are, the Bridge of Light over the darkness that illuminates the dark night of the soul and that you can see because of the darkness… I remember… I AM… I AM LOVE!

In this context, I am going to share with you 3 exercises of Shadow Work as a tool you can use even daily if you want when you identify a shadow.

Transmuting the Shadow Exercise

You lie down on the floor and you enter in a process of recognition of the shadow you want to transmute. You visualize it underneath the body like a black, pulsing magnet shape like your body as if you were lying over it.

You visualize this magnet extracting the poisonous black shadow and leaving your being… into the arms of Divine Mother Earth, you surrender the shadows to her to be transmuted…

You can stay there for 15 minutes or more until you feel a shift in your energy or a subtle change and you visualize a golden light body over you. You remain lying on the floor. This is the Divine light itself pouring golden light into you. Stay with it another 15 minutes or more and then write down your experience.

If you do this with sincerity and devotion, it can be a very healing and empowering exercise.

Cleaning Up Exercise

Ken Wilber is a scholar of the Integral stage of human development and the developer of an integral "theory of everything" that embraces the truths of all the world's great spiritual, scientific and philosophical traditions. He is often called "the Einstein of consciousness studies."

There is also a bridge I do with Wilber's work of Evolutionary Dynamics and Integral Life. He goes through the stages of becoming a Whole Being through Waking up, Growing up, Cleaning up and

Showing up—integral frameworks, fully aware of all the dimensions of our existence.

In the "cleaning up" part we do the shadow work when we:

1. Accept our shadow
2. Talk to it
3. Own it profoundly
4. Embrace it to transcend it

Anger Release Exercise

If necessary, depending on the client, and always customizing the sessions depending on the needs and unique situation of each person, I guide the process and we can also work with a beautiful and intense three-step exercise from Torah, a beautiful angel (energy of consciousness) that I worked with (and about whom I will tell you more about in Chapter Seven, which has to do with those unseen friends that reside in the invisible world and are a loving presence that guide your life).

Torah's exercise for anger release goes like this:

You are working with all the power of your imagination, indeed!

You wrap yourself in a bubble of light in a room where you are alone and nobody can hear you. You can have some pillows, some towels and a bucket.

You "give the intent" or manifest the intention for doing healing work. Everything is allowed within this bubble of healing light, and you do not want to splash it outside of that bubble. You establish this before starting the work with the intention for healing.

It can also help to have 2 chairs. You will work with someone close to you with whom you need to release anger. It can be you in this moment in your life, or if you need to work with your inner child you establish that for yourself releasing your anger towards your father or mother. Remember that there is no limit for energy and your imagination of time and space. You can establish yourself with these tools in the past in the case you are working with your inner child, your teen self or a younger you.

So you sit in front of the other person and voice all your anger towards him or her. You can use the pillows to beat them up or strangle them using the towels.

So you feel your anger, shouting whatever improprieties come to you... this can last for as long as you want, the important thing is to feel it deeply, at a cellular level. When you are done shouting, crying or feeling exhausted, you stop for a moment.

Now you move on to step 2. You are laying down and resting, and you visualize the person you are working with. They say "Please forgive me! You are absolutely right, please forgive me!" Nothing else is said and you let yourself feel it, you feel the endorphins and you feel it also at a cellular level. Here also you can stay for as long as you want—the important part is to let yourself feel whatever shows up.

The third step of the process to imagine that person asking you: "What can I do or give you to remedy all the harm I did you?" You imagine that he or she gives you exactly what you want or need. You let yourself feel.

If you find yourself asking for something while still charged with anger, you need to go back to step 1. It's OK. You can do it again until you let go. You can deepen all you want—I can tell you that it took me over 3 years of constant iterations of this exercise to release my anger towards my mother.

It is a very effective tool to release the chronic anger that lurks in the dark of your being, that powerful shadow that sabotages your spiritual growth.

Bridges of Light: Modules 5 and 6

We are ready now to go to **Module 5 – Bridge of Light with Infinite Self.** We work with the next Master activation of the Spirals of Freedom by Peggy to continue to strengthen our UCL and we bridge this energy work of this energy modality with introducing meditation into the equation… and maintaining, as always, the spiritual journaling.

Again, here we have 12 sessions that are our customized guided tools to continue our expansion of consciousness.

Here I introduce the Practice of No Problem or the Practice of Conscious Contentment as an indispensable element to access the Infinite Self. This meditation can be a floating element in whatever module, even starting with the first module if the person is already familiar with meditation.

Craig Hamilton is a spiritual trailblazer whose approach to transformation is bringing enlightenment down to Earth and unlocking the codes to our highest human potential through various courses. He is also a founding member of Ken Wilber's Integral Institute and a member of the Evolutionary Leaders Forum.

For me it has been a refreshing element after 10 years practicing Buddhist meditation and having retired from it for another 10. My re-encounter with meditation through workshops and practice with Craig Hamilton first and then resuming with Jeff Carreira in the Mystery School have been a joy and allowed me to re-integrate meditation as an indispensable element in my spiritual life on a daily basis, accompanied by contemplation and journaling (the other pillars of my daily practice).

This is what I introduce in this module for those who have not yet integrated this practice into their lives.

The Bridge of Light I was making with meditation became very obvious to me when I read Jeff Carreira's *No Place but Home: Reflections on Meditation and the Spiritual Life.*

He says "I believe a human being is a flow of divine energies and the aim of spiritual work is to open to and align with the flow of divine energy in the most creative, constructive, beautiful and beneficial ways possible." In the same book, he also says: "The ultimate goal of our practice is to allow a new and larger sense of self to emerge within us that can expand the possibilities of reality. If you hold this context for meditation your practice will be fueled by a very powerful energy source."

Additionally, "when you embrace the way things

are, exactly as they are, you simultaneously allow the energy of possibility to move through you. As a result your life changes in unimaginable ways because you are no longer striving to fix what is wrong and over-come limitation, you are now driven by possibilities that constantly invite you to realize them."

The true journey is the evolution of consciousness, and this is becoming the Bridge of Light you have al-ways been... Jeff continues: "as we learn to allow the larger journey of spirit unfold through us, we discover what we are here for."

This has been real for me since I started my own journey into the light and has been reinforced, deep-ened and mostly inspired all the way from when I re-started my meditation practice. As with the rest of the practices I want to share with others, which have brought me many benefits and allowed me to con-tinue my spiritual journey, they needed to be included as part of the building block that this module is in my body of work, to continue the magnificent journey of conscious evolution.

In his book, Jeff also says that "when we let go of any attempt to be anywhere other than here, all of our energy is available to do the invisible work of con-scious evolution. This is an endeavor worthy of devot-ing our life to. This is the journey we were born for. Can you imagine any love greater than this?"

Now, we are at **Module 6 – Bridge of Light with Multidimensional Self.**

Energetically, we work with another of Peg-gy's Master Activations—Imagine: Evolutionary

Timelines. This is another modality of the energy work that we bridge in the 12 sessions that are our tools in our evolutionary process, with the somatic work. We continue, as always, using spiritual journaling, which in these sessions will emphasize our imagination and will continue to expand our UCL.

We have established at this point of the process that we are wise, wholehearted, multidimensional beings in the energy and wisdom of Infinite Love. As Peggy says: "This Master Activation Series will activate new abilities to consciously choose and skillfully set new timelines. In the frequencies of these new abilities, we can co-create our realities, personally and collectively, with the clarity and focus required for these evolutionary vibrational and transformational times."

Susan Kullman is a spiritual life coach, somatic educator, yoga therapist and author that empowers others to live a life of intentional health and wellness. Susan is a resident teacher in the Mystery School, where I met her, and she offers weekly videos on transformation and somatic awakening. She also offers a live monthly somatic movement class, as well as courses and retreats. We bridge this energetic work with Susan's work of somatic awareness, emotional healing and spiritual awakening.

All the while, we continue—as always—using our spiritual journaling to anchor the revelations and dive deeper, continuing to bring forward the main theme in all of our Modules: becoming a Bridge of Light to bring more of our divinity to our everyday lives here on planet Earth and contribute with our co-creators to build new possibilities for a new paradigm for living in peace and beauty.

This is a journey, unfolding as my own evolutionary process as a Bridge of Golden Light continues. I will keep sharing the new bridges that develop as the series of revelations and discoveries in this sacred process called life.

As of now, this is what I offer:

Body of Work – Bridges of Light

- Module 1 – Bridge of Light with Inner Wisdom (EMF Balancing Technique®)
- Module 2 – Bridge of Light with Essence (Emergence: From Ego to Essence)
- Module 3 – Bridge of Light with Universal Self (52 Codes for Conscious Self Evolution)
- Module 4 – Bridge of Light with Whole Being (Shadow Work)
- Module 5 – Bridge of Light with Infinite Self (Meditation)
- Module 6 – Bridge of Light with Multidimensional Self (somatic awareness, emotional healing, spiritual awakening)

The modules comprise 12 sessions each. These sessions are one-on-one wither virtually or in person, though starting from Module 2 they can also be given in small groups.

The frequency of the attendance to the sessions is customized depending on the person or the group. This is valid also for all the trainings, workshops and classes that are included in the body of work.

I want to share a testimony that a client of mine in a year-long program shared with me in a letter.

It is incredible how the human being, in his spiritual awakening, searches for the path and the signs emerge in incredible ways.

That is how one day I heard the word "balancing." Someone said it had helped her, and the word resonated with me so I searched online and the name Adriana Colotti Comel came up. I called her and put myself in her hands, just trusting as I really did not know what it was all about. That was the beginning of many discoveries in a beautiful stage of my life.

For some time, I had already had the word "healer" in my mind. Something moved within me with that word; I'd studied many areas of mental and holistic health, but when I arrived at the EMF Balancing Technique®, specifically in Adriana's hands, I woke up.

In her care, step by step, day by day, with the work we did together I discovered the marvel of becoming a Bridge of Light and connecting with the divine in me and the wonderful wisdom of the Universe. Not only that: I discovered my potential when I worked with all of my senses. I learned to listen to my inner voice that is always there and that many times we ignore: intuition.

One amazing thing was discovering that I am a linker of worlds and the beautiful labor that this entails.

Without a doubt, I recognize that all people have unlimited connections with our Higher Self and when we turn our eyes inwards and learn to listen to that voice, it fills us with wisdom and becomes a very important guide to go beyond and enter the world of multidimensionality.

Of course it is a great endeavor to beat the incredulity, the fear to make mistakes, recognize our false beliefs and eradicate them from our lives, fly on the wings of love and forgiveness and mainly forget about looking with a magnifying glass at the person in front of us and ourselves. And the most important thing: to trust.

Infinite gratitude to Adriana Colotti.

My recognition to you and the beautiful work you do.

With love, Nidia

The Journey Unfolding

Brilliance is brighter
The golden light is stronger
The influx of light is huge
We are the receiver end
To reflect even more intensely
The love of our human hearts
To the blossoming of a new consciousness
For a new earth
Creation is afoot
We are getting closer to our divinity
With our evolutionary eyes
Jumping into the unknown
Of the mystery of life
Resonance is the key.

CHAPTER SEVEN

The Multidimensionality

———

I am sharing with you now the reality of unseen friends that have been and continue to be an inspiring guidance for my earthly life and for bridging it with the Divine. I hope you remember that in a previous chapter I told you the story of my Divine Dragon of the Light and how I brought forward the affirmation and prayers that have brought me here all along.

Kryon has been another important influence in my spiritual life.

Torah has been an unseen friend for many years now and as I translated him into Spanish here in Mexico I developed a close relationship with both him and Shawn throughout various workshops I've participated in with her.

Shawn also channels another entity called Ralio. Before I started to write this book, I got beautiful confirmation from him after asking specifically for guidance concerning this project. That gave me confidence and validation, as dialogues with invisible friends always do, always loving and empowering messages, guidance and orientation… in this case, Ralio said (through Shawn) answering my question:

> *The bridges are ready to be crossed, do not stall, keep on going with courage and passion, your passion splashing your light everywhere… jump, jump, jump, let your spiritual action be your traction, stand up for love, unmask your being, a Bridge of Golden Light, with self-responsibility, co-create a new possibility, adapt and be flexible, appreciate your growth and greatness, and continue forward with a smile in your heart. You are dearly loved! Infinite Gratitude!*

Within this context I will now continue to offer to you blessed guidance and dialogue with the Frequencies of Golden Light that speak to me profusely.

You live in a multidimensional reality! You are never alone! You are dearly loved!

Your journey included various guides, from the Divine Dragon of the Light, which grounded you with an extraordinary balance of masculine and feminine energies, to the follow-up of Kryon of Magnetic Service, which you devotedly followed up reading all the books. You even translated Kryon into Spanish for the first time in the American continent in Miami, Florida. A dimension opened there clearly. You felt the warmth of home and made a very revealing "mistake" when you translated "winds of earth" instead of "winds of birth." It was hardly a mistake… someone said the translation sounded like a jazz trio between the voice of Lee Carroll

(Kryon's channeler), the music of Robert Coxon that always accompanied him and your own melodious voice.

This opened for you a portal into the channeling world. You did not need to go to the presentations: everything you read and listened to talked directly to you and expanded your consciousness, bridging dimensions of understanding of yourself and the world as multidimensional realities, blending, intersecting, interweaving and opening those portals of the in-between worlds where you land when you journal and which you visit daily in your contemplations.

There is that straight connection of automatic writing with the invisible knowing of the presence of the beyond to ease your mind and pour into writing the wisdom of the ages, the dancing with spirit and the whispers of the soul.

The wonder of your friend Torah, who taught you about channeling in a workshop with trance channel Shawn Randall. You so enjoyed translating Torah into Spanish for Shawn's clients, as this made you stay very awake and develop a relationship with him that has endured through the years, even helping you with the healing in your own sessions with all the difficult relationship stuff. This evolved into a luminous presence of Source as you worked with Torah in your personal sessions and the translations for Shawn. You transcended limits and bridged dimensions as you directly listened to Torah bringing the clear and sound messages to the person involved in the session.

Through Torah you discovered your connection with Cascade, your own Higher Self connection. The cascading in and out of inspiration and revelations that culminated in a very rich jungle. This crystalline experience developed and expanded in your channeled journaling writing experience that paired with Ezequiel, your guardian angel that has been present as a masculine energy in the huge rock in the middle of the river, where you met with him and Cascade. This was the platform for climbing the stairs to heaven into multidimensional dimensions to have many adventures together.

Communications, as with Kryon, were direct. You heard all of them clearly speaking to you. You asked and had conversations with Torah as you would with a very good friend who poured wisdom into you for the very difficult situations you found yourself in, dealing with your personal relationships… You were never alone!

When you met with Tobias a very loving presence channeled by Geoffrey Hope, you started your spiritual poetry after translating for Peggy for many years during which you really practiced being a translator of energy. Peggy channeled Ahnya and you translated that energy into Spanish at the beginning of your EMF path, which continued for more than 20 years… as did your very close relationship with Peggy that is still alive today.

The Bridge of Light that you identified when working with Barbara Marx Hubbard in Conscious Evolution expanded with your Evolutionary Bridges that then fully evolved into the body of work as Bridges of Golden Light.

They are not linear paths, not really bound by time or space. They are dimensions that interweave with your current life in the 3D world only as a reference.

When, after many years, you revisited the channeling experience with Torah, there was a distinct shifting and raising of the energy where the Frequencies of Golden Light talked to you. You were reassured by Jeff when he validated for you what you already knew, that the energy can talk to you, and during a retreat with him you very clearly saw the cover of Bridges of Golden Light–Multidimensional experiences–My Piece of the Cosmic Puzzle. Long before you began journaling in your Van Gogh sketchbook, it was clear that that would be the cover of the book.

It's as if by magic: always guided, discovering the path and the writing more than planning it. The guidance is very subtle: it is a sensing that becomes clearer when you automatically without any interference of programming take dictation, so to speak, of that guidance, wisdom, clarity and love that shows up as written pages with all the answers you need for doing "life." This journaling has been going on for more that 40 years now and has evolved into a wonderful way of being in this world... but not from this world.

Your multidimensionality is your true nature and has always been. The book allowed you to review all the journals and summarize the interweaving of threads to be illuminated and integrated by the Frequencies of Golden Light that continue to manifest as the development of the soul path towards the Divine itself. Now we are exploring new territory with the dive into cosmic consciousness that will bring about even more refined Bridges of Golden Light with the tools you have and continue to develop, as well as amplifying the understanding of the Cosmos having a human experience.

Multidimensionality will continue to evolve and unify all these dimensions into the Divine Unity where you reclaim the power of the Energy of Infinite Love, indeed!

There are many states of consciousness you have explored,

represented as spaces of the soul where you abide and revisit the call for unity of dimensions. This was meant to be: it was your fate and destiny, you will create reality as you chose to continue to engage with your multidimensionality.

Sorting out the layers of conditioned patterns from society, family, religion and else you release them and choose to passionately engage with Spirit in the path of cosmic consciousness where there is only spiritual freedom as the beginning of the journey for the continuing development of the soul.

Once you are done with the restricted self, there is only a path forward from here towards the union with the divine and a feeling of urgency to bring clarity to the table here and now. No more wasting time on stupid games of engagement with ephemeral endeavors. The need of the hour is a total conscious commitment to bring more of the Frequencies of Golden Light into this multidimensional reality.

You've known passionate love and now the warmth of our frequencies of life and eternal love are the ones that prevail through the ages as always. Like the unending tides in this home of yours in the Cosmos, our souls tide in and tide out in an ocean of clear wisdom accumulated through the ages.

There are infinite experiences in a cosmic field of consciousness. They come through and continue to generate a multitude of expressions: the infinite exploring itself to expand that consciousness of wholeness without limits. The interconnections between dimensions are infinite: the weaving of lattices upon lattices as building blocks of truth upon truths of evolving wisdom and dances of light that emerge on the other side of the black holes creating universes and novelties never seen in the ocean of time.

In the darkness of space there is no death, there is only life in the darkness, expansion in awareness, the container of the infinite... what a paradox indeed!

You can find all the secrets of the universe in the flow and move of breath in and through your own body and the trillion cells that conspired to be together in this moment.

You are dearly loved!
Infinite Gratitude!

Tapestry of Life

There is a tapestry of my multidimensional ways through all my life:

The way of the shaman

The way of the energy worker

The way of the Buddhist meditator

With creative flows of practices that interweave all along:

The practice of the sociologist

The practice of the artist with theater, ceramics, writing

The practice of the creator, writer, new paradigm shifter, cultural creative

With the vision and the practice as the content and the context all along.

The Journey of the Soul/The Beginning

As a bridge of golden light
That comes from the center of divinity
And radiates through as a spark

To a lifetime that is a small dot
Of the infinite fireworks that come from beyond
Into this reality
And happens to have a name….
We meet on the bridge of light that spans be-
tween the worlds
Tracing the spark in infinity
Multiple universes, galaxies and stars
As a shooting star in reverse
Up and down the Milky Way
Jumping dimensions
Dancing with the stars
The soul tickles with joy
The heart smiles
The flickering flame of a candle
Moves with the wind of time
Drums as heartbeats in a huge circle
At the bottom of the valley
Around the sacred fire
In loving anticipation
Of the journey of the soul
Together!

I Am the Cosmos having a human experience, and
the Cosmos trusts me and loves me for being the conduit available for this world to know more of itself
and express and contribute divine light through me. A
magnificent Bridge of Golden Light that shines greatly with the frequencies of higher dimensions where
the glimmering and tingling of crystalline liquid light

forms and pours into this vehicle allowing the divine to unfold through.

Quoting Jeff Carreira as an inspiration for the understanding of what it means for me to be a Bridge of Light: "Spiritual freedom is one half of spiritual work. In that work we awaken to an inherent oneness that reveals the perfect potential of our essential being. You could say it gives us a glimpse of heaven and a vision of our highest possibilities."

He continues: "the other half of spiritual work is aimed at embodying our higher potentials. This involves both a mysterious inner ascension into more consistent abidance in heaven, and the effort to manifest more of heaven in our life here on earth."

Being a Bridge of Light goes both ways: to heaven and back to the marketplace, like the ten ox-herding pictures often used to describe the Zen path to enlightenment. They are folk images accompanied by poems and commentaries. They depict a young ox herder whose quest leads him to tame, train and transform his heart and mind, a process represented by subduing the ox and returning to the marketplace.

Daily Rituals and Invisible Friends' Support

For many years now, I've had daily affirmations/prayers/statements that I say aloud as active invocations, calls and conversations with the invisible realms.

Invariably, they always begin thus:

From the radiating core of my Infinite Self…
I ask my dear beloved divine essence

Bridging with my Universal Self
Being the whole being
To lovingly talk to me now
To be with me the whole way

Then I add a healing affirmation:

I radiate love in thought, words and deeds. I am a source of blessings. God and me, me and God, are one.

I continue:

Bridges of Light, I am with you. I ask you, my dear, beloved, divine bridges of golden light, to communicate with me now!

I am sharing this with you because I believe it is important for you to do your own research and discovery of whom you invoke every day and from where you want to live your day. And yes, it is a daily effort, a daily task, a daily confirmation of your connection with the Divine in whatever form you choose to do it. I complement it with oracles, tarot, astrology, numerology… special tools I've found that speak to me as I ask and I am open to receiving answers.

This affirmation is always accompanied by a visualization. I walk through a beautiful forest, enjoying nature; I come out into a clearing and there I wait and look towards the woods. My Higher Self shows up: a beautiful lady in a white, luminous gown. We embrace and she takes me to another opening in the woods, where I meet with the Frequencies of Golden Light that speak to me. I sit on a bench by the river where I let the Sun's rays shimmering on the water, the glittering golden light, transport me and show me the way and the guidance I need. Of course, by now

I am already journaling: there may have been a specific question, or sometimes just "What do I need to know?" And the journaling flows easily, sometimes for 10, 15 minutes, sometimes less or longer, no pre-planning and no boundaries or expectations. The feeling after that, however long it took, is always a peaceful, clear mind and an open heart with which I can go on with my day.

Over the many years that I have done and continue doing this, it has developed and deepened, and it has taken me into wonderful adventures, breakthroughs, and deep Shadow Work as needed. It inspires me, guides me and helps me go through life as the Cosmos having a human experience.

I cannot emphasize this enough: it is important to have your own rituals and the consistency of everyday connection with the invisible realms, friends, soul, angels, spirits or whatever you want to call them. This is what allows you to have a spiritual life and lead a wonderous human life no matter what.

Of course, a daily practice of meditation goes hand-in-hand with the contemplation and the journaling. Magical ingredients for a magical life on Earth to become the beautiful Bridge of Light we all are, indeed!

From the core of everlasting peace where you rest
Then you come back into the world with love
and innocence
For a new beginning
For the future of our world
As a brilliant light bringing possibility and hope

Resonating with Higher Vibrations

Resonating with higher vibrations of the awakened Cosmos, where soft winds of change blow eternally with the speed of light. We are showered by trillions of stars as dots of brilliant light coming through us as we merge with awakening consciousness through eons of time in the expansions of being one with the Cosmos.

The peace and emptiness of the freedom within that comes from vibrating with higher frequencies of light. Golden glimmering, vibrant light as the pool percolating through the multi-universes reaching a blue planet that is our temporary home where in resonance we meet through the expansive feeling of sacred space, shaped as our body of light that materializes as us human beings. The expression of the dream of the source of creation in luminous colored expressions of frequencies in a unique concert of united selves!

The Unfolding

The energy of love is the one ingredient that is present all the time during your explorations into your multidimensionality. It is driven by your love for the divine and it is encountered always beyond the obvious and ordinary reality. Another way to say this is that the universe is always speaking to you, if you allow it and pay attention.

For me, the avoidance of the power of love arises when I pretend that I am betrayed. Betrayal is really your betrayal to yourself and to knowing that the only unconditional love there is comes from your Higher Self—not from the ego, the small self. But the point is not to demonize the ego or the small self: that is why we work with our shadows, embracing them to be able to illuminate them and dissolve them.

So the blame, the judgement, the pretense of reciprocity of unconditional love from your fellow humans is the avoidance of your power and your responsibility of knowing that unconditional love comes from your Higher Self—you do not demand it from your fellow humans. When you confront them with that, it will only show their own lack of love for themselves, projected onto you. This is the entanglement!

So here come the Bridges of Golden Light, called by me to enlighten the process of love…

We are adjusting! In the brilliance of the light, there is a bandwidth that is expanding now: the bandwidth of the energy of love. The old frequencies of doubt and second-guessing yourself are diminishing in the light of trust of the Divine, so you can live content no matter what. You do not have to feel great or ecstatic each moment of the day, you let your humanness flow with all the nuances of being human knowing that the light is shining brightly even if there is a cloudy grey sky.

You've seen it in your flights, flying over a carpet of thick clouds with a vision of blue sky and brilliant Sun. The greenery you like so much reminds you of that Sun: chlorophyll production exists because it is the connection with the sunlight, this is the bridge between the stars and the Earth… you can see it in nature all around you.

you can hear the music of the spheres of Heaven and Earth

and all the planets, stars, asteroids in between, and if you go deeper you can hear the sound of distant galaxies reverberating through all the Cosmos and this is the reminder in the heart that all is one and the energy of love is all that is.

The intimacy is overwhelming. The light is bright as you take care of your human eyes so you can enjoy the radiation of Source. This is the love of the universe flowing through you, so you can radiate core light to all of your universe as you know it and beyond!

Sweet Essence, Water of Life, Darkest Cavern

Walking along a stream in the dark cavern... it is like a platinum ribbon of moonlight... it is the version of the liquid rainbow in the sunlight. In its sweetest essence, it reminds me of my brightness by the moonlight and the remembrance of a sacred garden where I drink the water of life that vibrantly brings me back to acknowledge that all is well in this chaotic world with multiple anxieties and decisions going wrong and not flowing smoothly. On the edge of losing my mind in a cosmic adventure through a black hole that I cross over and over each time I panic only to come out the other side, bathed in moonlight... another view opens up, reminding me that grace is restored.

Sometimes it feels like being in a blender and having it all mixed up just to see that you can breathe and all is well in the path to enlightenment and in the journeys into your multidimensionality. Here, Jeff's quotes from the book *Higher Self Expression: How to become an Artist of Possibility* are an inspiration and guidance to continue the journey. He says: "by cutting ourselves off from the subtle realms of the angels, we not only created an unbridgeable divide between us and God, but we also lost all connection with the means for inner growth." This is precisely what I am bridging and offering-inviting to be the Bridge of Light between us and God with the tools to build those Bridges of Light with others here on Earth with the teaching of living energetically aware.

Jeff continues: "angels of the imagination... perceive the soul of the world ... reveal the one fact of being... the ultimate being wants to be expressed in the world... genius is a spontaneous act of co creation." The language I use for this same thing is to be a Bridge of Light. You express and listen at the same time in this heavenly realms. He continues: "the imaginal realm, I see this beautifully evocative term as pointing to the same magical space of betweenness where the work of creative illumination takes place...

In order to engage in the imaginal realm we must develop the ability to perceive in multiple dimensions at once..."

This is my exploration in multidimensionality, I am sharing with you my story and the development of it all as I continue participating in the Mystery School and we continue to stabilize our platform to continue to go beyond individually and collectively. What an exciting journey this is! Infinite Gratitude!

In Jeff's words:

"Genius unsettles everything

We are building the path that we follow
We are reading the words as we write them
We are talking and listening at the same time…"

Dear Beloved Divine Bridges of Golden Light (here the Frequencies of Golden Light speak to me and I journal the message)…

From the mesmerizing light and glimmers from the flowing river we are beyond grateful and happy about our meeting, we want you to feel the gratitude and the love for all you have been doing and comfort you and reassure you that there is nothing wrong with how things are unfolding in your life. The mental expectations of an unreal thoughtful event where you expect things to be otherwise is the only obstacle to your happiness. What is and how it is perfect, you are perfect, reality is perfect. It should not be any other way, not even in your imagination. This is the process of co-creation where from the radical acceptance of what is you co-create with us and the rest of reality the next steps forward. There is no completion, there is a process of life unfolding, experiences after experiences and the feeling of "it should be different" is just another experience… it does not make it any better or worse, and you feeling that as a mistake is just another experience that has become a habit for you… so you can relax… with that too… All is well!

Interweaving the Multidimensional Threads of Life

So, as we are nearing the end of this journey we've embarked on together through all the threads that have been braided, woven, blended throughout this book, I find myself coming full circle. No beginning, no end in this multidimensional reality drawn in sacred joy from the start as the development has been revealed as a discovery while we have gone along with it.

My experience is like a script from the Cosmos: not only because of how the puzzle pieces of my poetry, my stories and my journaling have been put together, but also because I realize that such has been my life, I can perceive the ascendant process of Spirit present every step of the way. It all makes sense as this journey of my soul that is never-ending and continues to evolve and expand in luminous revelations, always puzzled together in a magical way with everyday realities.

I understand now that the timing of the book has been perfect. I needed to go through my mother's death to discover the ultimate Bridge of Golden Light: I feel she has been guiding and orienting me every step of the way for my ultimate freedom in this earthbound life. Everything we had not been able to share when she was here is now possible in these higher dimensions of being, where we meet in expanded states of consciousness without jeopardizing the pureness of our encounters with our human personality traits.

Torah, one of my invisible friends, helped me understand that these last months after her transition I have been releasing all the toxicity, the entangled dark chords, the serpents in a basket, which are entangled with the white chords that exemplify our human relationship between mother and daughter, characterized by love and hate.

Now the story is clearer for me. My mom felt released and finished her job here on Earth. She was tired and left. We were at peace, and I helped her transition.

She left so that now I could have a better life without worries and do what I need to do with my contribution to the world. I am watched over by the feminine divine mother guiding me every step that I take, and I can rest in this trust.

Ancestral Karmic disentanglement continues in a multidimensional way with all of my family, from whom I am now choosing to distance myself since these energies no longer contribute to my spiritual growth. Life is unfolding, I am releasing karma with the help of my unseen friends and I can tell you that you sure need courage to be an evolutionary human and a mystic in this days and age indeed!

And as Torah always says, Love is the strongest bridge between all dimensions. This is why the Bridge of Light with the energy of love is the one I will explore, experience and follow until the end of my days in this lifetime and beyond.

Disappearing

Stepping into The Divine
I become oblivious
I disappear
And…
I find myself in a hall of mirrors
There I see Other Eyes
Galaxies, streams of light, the Milky Way

All the wonders of the Natural World
Fires, Floods, Earthquakes,
The Sacred Silence in the Void
There is a puddle of water in the center of the
circle
It is a Mystery... Amen...

What is Next?

It is a new butterfly coming out of the cocoon
Shedding the old and slowly spreading its multicolored wings
to fly into the horizon
It reminds me of the flight on the back of my
Divine Dragon of the Light
when we came out of the bottom of the ocean
overflying into infinity...
I can see the energetic planetary grid
hovering above the quagmire of reality
as a parallel reality where I abide
where I discover my multidimensional
illumination
The intensity of the liquid fire is transformative
I am free to explore and willing to change forever
and come out the other side of the black hole as
a brilliant explosion of light
Isn't this the way stars are born?
In the beyond I find myself very still
Going back to the river flowing into the ocean
Floating again and letting the sunshine bathe me
It feels salty...
What is next?

With laser light attention I go to the bottom of
the experience to see clearly
Highest possibilities!
Habitual patterns blooming through the cracks
shape my experience
What happens if I do not move?
I can relax and flow… back to the river… float
in the ocean…
Enjoy the rotation of the Earth as the Sun is left
behind
I allow the universe to flow through me and I am
at peace!
I go beyond the conscious and the unconscious
where touching is a metaphor for the mind
engaging…
I am free!

Touching the Light

In the womb of Infinite Self
where my heart beats
I can hear the whispers of my soul
Reaching out to a cosmic experience
of expansion and awe
In the intimacy of stillness
The expansiveness of galaxies
Exists in the very fibers of my being
I reach a depth that rotates as a toroid
where here is there
and there is here
and the subtle is present
The chirps of birds

remind me of a wonderful planet
that is home for the Divine
for the time being.

Bewildered!

There was also The Mystery School writing circle that I participated in that helped a lot in my process of writing, not only my journals but my automatic writing to address the spontaneous articulation of what needs to be shared.

Here is one excerpt. I am quoting myself in the process:

There are less brilliant moments, of course. The reminders of explosive light are good as rechargers. Now, I can float and observe what is there and here and reconcile the disappointment, reinterpreting the truth of what is. The unfolding of what is written is impeccable, misunderstandings are adamant. Miscommunications are too. That is why the reminders are needed: so that we can make sense of it after sleepless nights looking for meanings. Clarity comes eventually. I'll let go of the illusion of success and find the gem of wisdom or care or love or not that shows itself in the bottom of the well...

We discover the letters of karma hidden in chaotic data revealing themselves as pieces of a cosmic puzzle indeed!

Yes... putting things in order... everything in is its

proper place... naming it with sincerity and truth for what it is. A process that is sometimes crude and real, when I feel hurt it is difficult for me to find gentleness or kindness. I am still too involved; I thought it would come out differently. But here we go again. It is a matter of having expectations and really nothing is as it seems for better or worse.

I can see more of his or her weakness and we mirror each other and as I idealize people and put them on a pedestal and when they show their true colors I cry, my stomach aches. Digestion is not easy. So I process and chew and then I chew some more.

I know that eventually I will have more clarity on what happened and why it happened the way it did. I wonder why it takes so long to realize, feel and sense all of the complex situation to get the pearl of wisdom. Again, it is what it is and that is OK! Even the impatience that appears while I am processing it, the writing, the understanding and the sharing... it is what it is... Indeed!

It is easier for me when I do it for others, surely because there isn't so much of me involved! I apply the reflection energetic tool core to core, do the technique, conduct the sessions with the necessary protocol and it never fails: the empowerment of the other person or group is achieved as a result of their inner wisdom and the Bridge of Light they are making.

It is also difficult to not get distracted with

irrelevances. It is bittersweet, and I stay in the bitter too long... until the sweet shines out.

I wish for it to be more expedited, and I know the only way is through it.

I have been bewildered these days, that's what was happening: I now recognize the pain, I was numb. Well... I'll put everything in its place and go forward. I did my best and I solved it. I was not counting on them pulling out. It hurt us both.

We all want to live a good life. If we allow simplicity, if we allow sincerity, kindness and love. If only we allow...

Everything is so confusing now. There are those in the transhumanistic movement that want to put chips in their brains to communicate with computers directly. They give the power to machines and artificial intelligence when we have not even begun to discover how magnificent our humanness is and that really we are the technology... so guess what: I will continue handwriting my journals and books. I will not renounce the pleasure of connecting my hand with my heart and filling up dozens of beautiful white-paged journals combined into a beautiful collage... Amen!

Bridging the Light

It's all a matter of bridging the light and meeting

each other in the middle. It is not a one-way street. As it is a multidimensional, intradimensional crossing, it becomes imperative to expand the bridging. There is no linearity in the process. You can just be present with all that is every moment, all at the same time.

Vulnerability, intimacy, we space, implications, what is present, so many shades of light... Relax and traverse the shades!

Is it a suspension, a floating feeling? How do we craft our everyday life with the immensity of possibilities?

Relax and let the excitement begin. No problem... all is well. Allow for perfect acceptance, open to whatever experience you are having. Perfect!

Lost in thought, disappointment, the illusion of been lost arising, no place to go...

Relax in total acceptance, fascinated by the movement of the mind. How it happens. Perfect vulnerability, unbroken. Open, receptive accepting to whatever arises. The momentum of vulnerability. The depth of receptivity, always.

Being where you are, not lost in the movement that bounces off a million faces.

Connecting, we meet in illuminated consciousness, freedom... the inside is what communicates.

The mesmerizing, the tingle, the brilliance, the golden light, the sparkling, yes!

The river flowing, the wind, the sparkling, the water, the liquid light. Eddies and whirlpools exist only in water, we are interdependent and interconnected. We are a manifestation of life, energetic experiences

of being. Basking in golden light, sunlight, warmth…
we are formed in life, no "me" to be removed, no separation, like the whirlpools in the water: you cannot
extract a whirlpool by itself, it exists because of the
water. We trust what we do not know.

The Journey of the Soul

We are having a ball
From the universe and back
You have always been a writer
From the beginning of times
Scrolling your Dharma
On the sheets of existence
Writing along
This is the journey of your soul
This is the joy of your heart,
The universal files of experience
In a multi-universe of choice
Your way of relating and communicating
Now, time to share it
To empty the files
As we are getting ready
For the next big adventure of this lifetime
Indeed!

It is a jigsaw puzzle I am putting together, assem-
bling all the pieces already there. The book is done.
Now, I am forming it into a comprehensive structure
for the reader to go through and find the pearls of wisdom to have their own experiences of awakening as I

share my own, so they can enjoy the invitation to be a Bridge of Light in their own life and the life of others.

We are building new possibilities together.

So yes, this is my piece of the cosmic puzzle. Bridges ready to be crossed!

So excited and so greatly loved!

Infinite Gratitude!

Indeed!

Love

The heartbreak is of the heart. Pain is unbearable and one can die. The romanticism era of artists showed us that. There is a bandwidth of emotions that is new now: it goes from the infrared to the ultraviolet. It is extreme and you have to hold the tension and bridge it. I say bridge the light of the divine into daily life, bridge the light with our co-creators to be able to build a more enlightened life from the first contact so we can be Bridges of Light for the world, transforming our thoughts and perceptions, speaking differently. Our choices in action reflect a new paradigm in which we would all want to live with an open heart. There is abundance of love to go around.

What does it mean to live wholeheartedly?

To hold it all, the pain and the suffering, but also to ask ourselves how much joy and happiness we can hold. Nobody teaches us that, or why we make pain a priority. To hold joy and even laughter until you belly hurts, how sporadic is that?

I insist: we should be able to expand the bandwidth

of emotions and live wholeheartedly and multidimensionally a free range of emotions to discover a universal freedom that allows us to have a radical acceptance of the cosmic jokes constantly showing up if we allow a little expansion and humor into our rusted perspective of a very small world where stubbornness frankly sucks.

Are we doomed or are we going to allow nature to grow in its beauty and harmonize with the mutual needs we share with a planet that is hurting and crying out loud that it needs its inner heart to be heard?

The beatings of the inner Earth that are felt on the surface are cries of pain. We should listen, open our hearts more until they can beat in unison with every living tree and every living species that makes up the rainbow tapestry of this wondrous planet that we inhabit as the only home—which, by the way, is for now the only home we have in the Cosmos. We are earthbound for now and we can learn, learn to love more as a species that risks extinction if it doesn't understand how to live wholeheartedly.

What a paradox, indeed!

A warm cozy feeling of togetherness permeates the space where we are in the middle of the ethers. So spacious, so wide, so free of debris.

What a miraculous ground to play together.

And, as Torah says: Love is the strongest bridge between dimensions. I received confirmation from Torah that Mom is OK. He said that she never left my heart, from the very beginning until the very end… and now, beyond.

...you are that, it is consciousness, divinity flowing through you in a unique way. Mom is the same consciousness she was and is now. you were close, karmic families.

Yes, you had your life and she was always part of it, as she still is... though in presence no more. It is another kind of presence. She is with you and wants you to have a good life. She wanted to go. She lost vital force in her body. Her body did not respond to her. She was leaving the body. The Universal Mother explains Mom: you continue your life with her support as always, just not present in the body and in this space anymore. You are going to consummate now the Bridge of Light between you two.

There are the realms of the soul where angels abide and you two are one in the light of divinity.

You bring that light down here where needed, to your daily life.

It is a clear sky, a brilliant Sun shining strongly. Awareness of spirit is bright, winds of freedom blow.

To be continued...
In Love and Light!

Epilogue

———

The process to write the book has been brought to me as subtle guidance each step of the way: the spiritual poetry inspired by daily guided meditations with Jeff Carreira in The Mystery School, the encouragement of their publication in *The Artist of Possibility* magazine, the meditation retreats and Jeff giving me confidence by telling me that energy can very well be talking to me... all that journaling through all these years, the reviewing, classification and codification of all my journals starting in 1983 non-stop to this day with the practice of writing the channeling, contemplations and inspirations from Spirit and my soul dialogues that guided me all the way and continue to do so.

I feel blessed to be able to translate the energy, put it into words... and in English, so strange! My native language is Italian by birth (and Spanish by place of birth), but all my spiritual life, starting with Zen Buddhism, has been in English.

A virtual course with Christine Kloser called *Get Your Book Done* helped me cover the basic initial questions and intents to shape the book, and it also taught me the card technique (randomly writing points, ideas, comments and whatever else on cards, each of which became a piece of a cosmic puzzle all over my apartment floor). The columns of content started to make sense together as I reordered them in a sequence, turning each column into a chapter to sort out the specifics for each. I captured the information on an excel sheet and then printed it out as a huge scroll that had the basic structure of the book' content laid out.

All of my beautiful, artistic sketch books in which I continue write with my purple liquid gel ink pen sliding over the white sheets were quickly filled with text. They then underwent a color-coding, posting, selection process so I could easily locate in the more than 13 of them the information I needed to complete certain pages of the book with specific quotes or poems written in time that fit in the whole puzzle putting together process of this multilayered facets of bringing this book together.

A multidimensional manifestation of the Bridges of Golden Light guided me through the whole journey. A gift from Spirit translated into my soul into words to be expressed as a transmission to be shared with you, the reader.

I am deeply honored and humbled by this process, which has been life-changing for me... and I know this is just the beginning. Infinite Gratitude to all and to you, the reader, for making this sharing possible.

In the last stretch of the process, when my mom died, I could not write. I had just written the introduction and I could not do more, as the grief was so acute. It was then that the Mystery School offered a workshop with Amy Edelstein that I took, hoping to find my original intention for writing the book that I knew was there, deeply hidden from my conscious unwillingness to engage again. I was too depressed, devastated and angry, as I told you before.

After those six weeks of important revelatory work to find my "hero journey," during which we shared our writings with the other participants, I met Maria Decsy. I've had various interactions with other members of The Mystery School, always looking for a lasting spiritual friendship. Maria and I engaged in weekly one-hour sessions in a process that continues to this day, and it has given me the confidence to finish writing my book.

I share this with you as a reader for you to know, if you get inspired to write your own book, how important it is to be able to read out loud to a kindred soul what you write, to have their feedback as a reflection while you are radiating and mirroring your light core-to-core. Maria herself is a great teacher of comparative religion, ethics and philosophy in various universities, and when we meet we do so at a soul level that allows us to connect in a loving field where our interactions feed our souls.

Maria is also writing her own book, and our encounters have also been very inspiring for her. I can't emphasize enough how her listening and loving feedback gave me the confidence to finish the book—and how she also loved being an enlightened ingredient for its completion. Thank you, Maria, for your listening and compassion as the beacon of hope that you are. Infinite Gratitude!

My godchild has done an excellent job editing each chapter on-the-go, and she has been very helpful in the process of finishing the book so it can be submitted for publication.

Infinite Gratitude to The Mystery School for offering such a wonderful platform and being the container that facilitates spiritual growth with so many variants.

My infinite gratitude to Jeff Carreira for being willing to look at my book and offering to publish it, waiting for me no matter what. I would not have done it without this encouragement.

Completion and new beginnings in a year of huge transformation!

Celebration, indeed!!!

My Journals and the Divine Dragon of Light

Suggested Bibliography

Carreira, Jeff. *The Path of Cosmic Consciousness: A Practical Guide to Higher Dimensions of Reality*. Emergence Education, 2022.

Carreira, Jeff. *Higher Self Expression: How to Become an Artist of Possibility*. Emergence Education, 2021.

Carreira, Jeff. *The Path of Spiritual Breakthrough: From Awakening to Cosmic Awareness*. Emergence Education, 2021.

Carreira, Jeff. *No Place but Home: Reflections on Meditation and the Spiritual Life*. Emergence Education, 2020.

Carreira, Jeff. *Paradigm Shifting: Guiding Evolution from the Inside*. Emergence Education, 2017.

Carreira, Jeff. *The Miracle of Meditation: A Gradual Opening into Unbroken Trust*. Emergence Education, 2020 (2nd edition).

Carroll, Lee. *The Journey Home*. Hay House Inc., 1998.

Carroll, Lee. *The Twelve Layers of DNA*. Platinum Publishing House, 2010.

Edelstein, Amy. *Adventure in Zanskar: A Young Woman's Solitary Journey to Reach Physical and Metaphysical Heights*. Emergence Education, 2021.

Harvey, Andrew. *Radical Passion: Sacred Love and Wisdom in Action*. North Atlantic Books, 2012.

Kullman, Susan. *Commit to What Is: A guided workbook for building a revolutionary relationship with our emotions and ourselves*. Emergence Education, 2021.

Lipton, Bruce H. *The Biology of Belief: Unleashing the Power of Consciousness, Matter & Miracles*. Hay House Inc., 2016 (10th Anniversary Edition).

Marx Hubbard, Barbara & Anderson, Carolyn. *52 Codes for Conscious Self-Evolution: A Process of Metamorphosis to Realize Our Full Potential Self*. Awakened World Press, 2011.

Marx Hubbard, Barbara & Anderson, Carolyn. *52 Codes for Conscious Self-Evolution: A Process of Metamorphosis to Realize Our Full Potential Self* – SPANISH VERSION - (Translated by Adriana Colotti Comel.) (Kindle only) Awakened World Press, 2015.

Marx Hubbard, Barbara. *Conscious Evolution: Awakening the Power of Our Social Potential.* New World Library, 2015 (revised edition).

Marx Hubbard, Barbara. Emergence: *The Shift from Ego to Essence.* Hampton Roads Publishing Company, Inc., 2001.

McTaggart, Lynne. *The Field: The Quest for the Secret Force of the Universe.* Harper Perennial, 2012.

Phoenix Dubro, Peggy & Lapierre, David P. Elegant *Empowerment: Evolution of Consciousness.* Platinum Publishing House, 2002.

Walsch, Neale Donald. *Conversations with God* (3-book set). Hodder and Stoughton, 2017.

Wilber, Ken; Patten, Terry; Leonard, Adam & Morelli, Marco. *Integral Life Practice: A 21st-Century Blueprint for Physical Health, Emotional Balance, Mental Clarity, and Spiritual Awakening.* Integral Books, 2008.

Suggested Websites

Puentes de Luz (Adriana Colotti Comel). www.puentesdeluz. com.mx

Bridges of Golden Light (Adriana Colotti Comel). www.bridgesofgoldenlight.com

Emergence Education (Jeff Carreira). emergenceeducation.com

Jeff Carreira. jeffcarreira.com

Kryon (Lee Carroll). kryon.com

Peggy Phoenix Dubro. www.peggyphoenixdubro.org

Shawn Randall. shawnrandall.com

The Mystery School (Jeff Carreira). mysteryschool-memberscircle.com

About the Author

Adriana Colotti Comel is a first-time author, sociologist, ceramist, practitioner and teacher of energy psychology. Passionate of spiritual journaling and poetry writing, she loves to build bridges of light with others for a more enlightened life. She lives in Mexico City and is devoted to her soul development as an artist of possibility as she continues to articulate and share her discoveries of higher dimensions.

Made in United States
North Haven, CT
22 August 2023

40639997R00117